WARRIOR
in the
GARDEN

NOBUO YAGAI
with MIKE NINOMIYA

Blue Ocean Books

Warrior in the Garden
Published by Blue Ocean Books.

Yagai/Nobuo Author
Warrior in the Garden
Nobuo Yagai

ISBN 978-1-7337732-0-1

Book layout and design by e-book-design.com

Blue Ocean
BOOKS

2493 North Dallas St
Aurora, Co 80010
www.blueoceanbooks.org

This book is printed in the United States of America

Foreword

It is better to be a warrior in a garden than to be a gardener at war.
—Sun Tzu

In feudal Japan, the need for combat professionals was similar to the order of knights in European history. Samurai means to serve in combat in Japanese and they were a privileged class because of their power and authority. Virtue was necessary because of a warrior's ability to take a life. As with any professional standard of behavior, there were laws and regulations for controlling people. Yet the warrior's code of personal conduct was neither a law nor a written rule, but a way of being: the samurai way. Without order there would be chaos, but too much order stifled the heart. The goal was to find balance and the challenge for the samurai warrior, in the distant past and for all of us today, is to define and implement one's ethics on a day-by-day, or even a moment-by-moment, basis. Being a samurai now is not about how to wield a sword, but about how to transform one's self to live a better life.

The martial arts offer three transformational experiences. First, the individual must transform his physical potential by utilizing particular techniques and theories. Next, he must regulate his emotions in order to understand his strengths and weaknesses, and to work on any blockages holding him back. Finally, he must be able to transmit the spirit and essence of his art to others in a productive way. These principles were utilized in a practical way by Dr. Jigoro Kano who founded Judo as a physical, mental, and moral teaching in Japan in 1882.

Dr. Kano expressed the basic principle of a productive society as the "efficient use of one's energy and mutual prosperity to self and other." This was his version of the warrior code of Bushido at the end of the samurai era. He successfully blended the culture of Japan with the rest of the world in an accessible way. Not only was this beneficial for the Japanese identity, but it gained worldwide popularity still present today.

In much the way that Dr. Kano made a practical contribution, Professor Inazo Nitobe used another approach to achieve the same end: the concept of the "intellectual samurai sword" as a method to discover and live a productive life. It is not simply about combat, but a search for finding purpose within the self.

Professor Nitobe was born into a samurai family on September 1, 1862. He attended a school founded by an American Civil War Colonel, William Smith Clark, who spent eight months in Japan in 1874 establishing the Sapporo Agricultural College, later to become Hokkaido University. In America, he founded the University of Massachusetts. To this day, Clark is a notable figure in the history of Japan and on the island of Hokkaido, his quiet influence in keeping with his humble demeanor.

Professor Nitobe attended the school founded by Colonel Clark. In 1920, the professor served as deputy secretary general of the League of Nations and was instrumental in that body successfully negotiating the terms of a territorial dispute regarding the Aland Islands. Using the "intellectual samurai sword," he kept both countries from engaging in military confrontation.

In 1900, Nitobe wrote the book *Bushido: The Soul of Japan*, translated into over 20 languages, including English, making the spirit of the samurai available to people around the globe. Both Dr. Kano and Professor Nitobe were heavily influenced by the man widely known as "One of the last samurai," Katsu Kaishu. He orchestrated the bloodless surrender of Edo (Tokyo) and a peaceful transition in Japan in 1868, when a major war could have broken out and the country could have been divided and/or fallen apart.

Professor Inazo Nitobe and his wife Mary Patterson Elkinton.
© Nitobe Memorial Museum.

Bushido: The Soul of Japan was one of the first major works about Samurai virtue and Japanese culture. Among those who loved the book were President Theodore Roosevelt, the American inventor Thomas Edison, President John F. Kennedy, and the founder of the Boy Scouts, Robert Baden-Powell. President Roosevelt was so inspired by the book that he started taking private lessons from Yamashita, a Kodokan Jiu Jitsu/ Judo instructor.

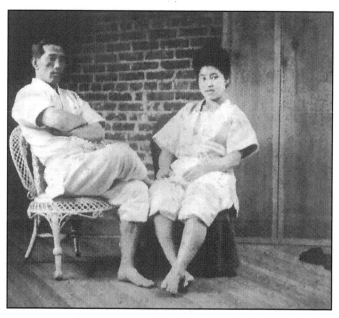

President Roosevelt's private instructor, Yoshitsugu Yamashita, and his wife.
© Kodokan Judo Institute.

A trusted Edison associate was Yoshiro Okabe, a Japanese-trained engineer and officer in the Japanese Imperial Navy. He contracted typhoid fever while his ship was stationed in New York. After recovering, he secured employment with Edison in Menlo Park, New Jersey. Okabe had studied the Bushido book and was a practitioner of Judo, impressing Edison with his character, integrity, courage, and loyalty. Using his martial arts skills, Okabe once drove off an attacker when Edison was being assaulted. The American inventor introduced Okabe to Henry Ford who took him on camping trips.

In 1905, President Theodore Roosevelt, who trained in martial arts three times a week at the White House, said, "The art of Jiu Jitsu is worth more than all of our athletics combined." His martial arts instructor was Yoshitsugu Yamashita, a pioneer of Judo in America, who also taught Roosevelt that discipline.

During the three stages of development in martial arts, which we will explore in this book, we must first become strong ourselves, both physically and emotionally, and then use our strength to help others. Our days on earth are limited, but when we use our energy wisely and efficiently, we can transcend time itself. Our essence can be transmitted through experience and education from the past to future generations—like a peaceful gardener planting seeds that will bloom in years to come. But planting a garden is just the first step. Next comes fertilizing, watering, and making certain that weeds don't harm the correct and fruitful growth. Like those plants, the self must be cared for fully and consistently.

We have minimal control over external circumstances, but we can see conflict for what it is and find a solution without creating more conflict—the goal of the warrior in the garden.

Introduction

As a young boy in Japan, I was raised in the traditional art of Kendo. Since then, I've been captivated by the never-ending journey of the martial arts and especially by the way of the samurai. This book is in appreciation for everything that journey has given me. In my youth, I was primarily attracted to finding tough opponents who tested my combat skills. Over time, I began to understand that martial arts aren't just about physical prowess, but how to deal with the mind and emotions, and how this develops our character.

Originally, I came to America for a special apprenticeship at the Enshin Karate dojo in Denver, Colorado. Having graduated from college in Japan, I wanted to challenge myself by venturing to a different country. I wanted to see if I had the discipline and structure to survive in the unknown. My journey deepened when I encountered the art of Jiu Jitsu, which emphasized softness to overcome brute strength. In Japan, Jiu Jitsu was recognized as an art that samurai used for close combat. On the battlefield, samurai who were without their swords or other weapons utilized this as a method to defend themselves. If they stumbled and fell to the ground, they kept fighting with body movements, using leverage to get better combat positions.

The literal Japanese translation is *jiu*, meaning gentleness, like the flowing of water, and *jutsu*, meaning art or skill. As I expanded my training, I realized there is more to Jiu Jitsu than skill on the mat, and I knew this would become my life path. In time, I encountered masters from the Gracie and Machado families, who are well-known in the martial arts community. The Gracies learned the art of Jiu Jitsu from Mitsuyo Maeda of Kodokan, the world Judo headquarters in Japan, and then improved upon it. A Gracie family member hosted the first UFC cage fighting competition in Denver, Colorado, and my mentor is Rigan Machado, a nephew of Carlos Gracie.

I began to appreciate how these skills could apply to any situation in life. They originated with Dr. Jigoro Kano and were developed through his student Maeda, aka Conde Koma, in Brazil. The more I learned about Jiu Jitsu, the more I wanted to understand Dr. Kano's samurai mindset.

Dr. Jigoro Kano (right), age 11, with his brother.
© Kodokan Judo Institute

Born on October 28, 1860, in Kobe, Japan, Dr. Kano would serve in the Japanese Ministry of Education and make powerful contributions to physical education. In 1882, he developed the art of Judo as an outgrowth of his own journey in Ju Jitsu. Judo, known as *Ju*, meaning "Gentle" and *Do* meaning "Way or Path." His study of *Ju Jitsu* and creation of Judo, which stressed merging mental skills with physical lessons, was his way of overcoming his smaller stature and sickly childhood. He was determined to transform what others saw as his weaknesses into strengths. In 1927, he founded Nada Junior/Senior High School in Kobe. The school adopted the mottos: *Seiryoku Zenyo,* meaning "maximum efficiency," with *Jita Kyoei,* meaning "mutual benefit." Dr. Kano worked as a servant for world peace until his last breath in 1938. In 1964, as part of his legacy, Judo was included as an Olympic competition.

The author with protector for Kendo.

My own martial arts journey began at age six with learning the ancient art of Kendo, the way of swordsmanship. I was inspired by the samurai of historical and feudal Japan and especially by Masamune Date, who has significant influence in today's Japan. A feudal warlord during the Sengoku period that lasted until 1603, he's a legendary figure in Japan. His open mind and fierce embrace of individualism made him an unconventional samurai and his visionary belief in internationalism was unique in feudal Japan.

Masamune's warrior armor, including a specially-created helmet, became the inspiration for the Darth Vader outfit in George Lucas's *Star Wars* films. Lucas was an executive producer on the Japanese film *Kagemusha* by the famous director Akira Kurosawa, a film inspired by Samurai General's double life. For *Star Wars*, Lucas was also influenced by the classic 1958 Japanese movie, *The Hidden Fortress*.

Masamune Date statue.

Masamune Date was part of the Tokugawa shogunate (1603-1868) that resulted in 250 years of peace in Japan. Masamune adopted the concept of *Bunbu Ryodo*, which required samurai to attain physical excellence and cultivate an artistic way of quieting the mind and the spirit. It included the Japanese arts of *shodo* (brush writing), *kado* (flower arrangement), and *sado* (tea ceremony). This was like juggling many balls while understanding the need to focus on those made of glass, which would shatter if they hit the ground. Perhaps the most fragile ball represents the inner self, which many of us fear the most to confront. The way of the warrior is to overcome the greatest weakness of the inner self and turn it into the most powerful asset.

Shy as a child, Masamune met an educator who taught him how to master Zen. One of his mentor's sayings was, "Clear your mind of all mundane thoughts and you will find even fire cool." As a little boy, I too was shy before taking martial arts training, which allowed me to transform myself and choose my own life.

Masamune lived in both the battlefield era and the Samurai peace era, so he needed a flexible mind. One time a samurai ruler was unhappy with Masamune not greeting him in the traditional ruler's way. Later, Masamune appeared before him in a white Kimono, a *hara-kiri* costume, which signaled his life's end. The ruler could have had him killed but admired his courage and left him unharmed. Masamune was tough-minded and unpredictable. He loved to cook, unusual for a samurai, but was confident enough not to worry about his time in the kitchen.

I was inspired not just by his cool Kabuto costume, but by how he lived and enjoyed himself along the way. He was both a great warrior and a good scholar, filled with wisdom. This concept of balancing one's life in this way is known as *Bunbu Ryodo*. His example has influenced how I've chosen to shape my own life.

The inner journey to understanding oneself is born and grows in the heart, spirit, and mind. The modern samurai has a primary goal of making the world a better place and seeking universal peace. The challenge of modern times is to not only maintain the ancient traditions, but evolve them in a way that fits the present day. Martial arts knowledge gives us the ability to make the best of a situation, no matter how unfortunate. Education is gathered information; knowledge is the power to select the correct information and take the right steps.

Life is precious and overwhelmingly beautiful. But it is also short, like the cherry blossom. In Japan, the blossoms are representative of the wonder and the fragility of life. They peak around two weeks into their existence and then begin to fall to the ground. The cherry tree encourages one to live in the moment and follow one's convictions with determination. In realizing our own vulnerability, we become more sensitive to this in others, both on and off the battlefield.

More than 100 years have passed since Professor Nitobe's time, but Bushido remains influential, not only in Japanese culture, but collectively in the business world, in art, in cooking, and in the sports world. In writing this book, I feel compelled to explore Professor Nitobe's concepts for today's students and to share tools that develop inner strength and allow an individual to follow his or her own path.

The samurai understood the way of the warrior, but the modern expression of Bushido requires adding the element of love. This was traditionally not associated with samurai, because in wartime love created too much vulnerability. Today, the idea of love goes beyond benevolence. It becomes an act of devotion and is unconditional in inspiring the warrior to fight for something larger than himself and to engage in productive work with compassion. Love will enhance your dreams and deepen your purpose in giving back to society.

While I was traveling to Colorado Springs in April 2016 with Master Rigan Machado, he suggested I write about my modern journey of living between cultures and bringing the way of the warrior into the contemporary world. An extremely open-minded Jiu Jitsu master, Rigan seeks to connect the martial arts to different communities and to share it with celebrities. Initially, writing a book in English when Japanese was my first language seemed like a far-fetched idea. But after hearing these challenging words, I felt a surge of excitement about a project that's also an expression of the way of the samurai. An effort to capture and share the history, culture, tactics, and philosophy of the samurai took hold of my imagination.

A famous samurai once served the feudal lord clan (Amako family), along with Shikanosuke Yamanaka (*Shika* in Japanese means deer). He was well known for his bravery and one-on-one combat skills. Shikanosuke was challenged by a samurai named Okaminosuke (*Okami* means wolf) claiming that he would overcome the deer. After two hours of fighting that may have included Okami using a bow, swordsmanship, and grappling, Shikanosuke prevailed. The Amako samurai observers cheered and said, "The deer won. The world is in delight." All the while, Shikanosuke became famous as much for his kindness as his fighting skills. He knew that all obstacles and challenges in life made for strength and growth—spiritual growth as well as self-improvement. The evolution of one-on-one combat, with its earliest beginnings during the samurai period, is today known as UFC and other similar events. We can experience video games such as Street Fighter II, demonstrating the concept of fighters challenging opponents from different disciplines, in order to compete and to prevail in the right way, the way of the Bushido code. I now offer a new examination, for today's world, of Bushido and vulnerability and love.

Chapter 1

The Way of Life

*W*hat is Bushido?

Roughly translated, it is Japanese chivalry. More than this, it was the unwritten code that the warrior observed to carry a sword with responsibility. Martial arts can be used negatively if the correct mindset is not established. Every situation is different and requires one to feel what is correct or not. For this reason, the code was not written out in a formal way. Professor Nitobe was the first to break down the code in a practical framework in written language. In honoring his spirit, I have followed his framework, but with a more modern emphasis.

Once we understand why a warrior needs a code, and why it must be applied to a specific situation, we can address the issue of right and wrong. As a simple example, we tell kids in class not to push others inappropriately; but if a person is about to be hit by a car, pushing him toward safety can be appropriate. Understanding this distinction comes from empathy and is related to your heart—where intelligence and the choice between good and evil exist. Dr. Kano based his philosophy on *jita kyoei* (mutual prosperity). He used the example of telling a lie to a violent person who asked, "Where are the kids hiding?" in order to protect their lives.

The ancient daoist philosopher Mencius believed in the natural goodness of people. Known as Meng Ke, he's often referred to as the "Second Sage" of Confucianism. In China, he was known as Mengzi, meaning Master Meng. His example of a child standing by a well is stated this way: "Suppose someone suddenly saw a child about to fall into a well. Anyone in such a situation would have a feeling of alarm and compassion—not because one sought to get in good with the child's parents, not because one wanted fame among one's neighbors and friends, and not because one would dislike the sound of the child's cries. From this we can see that if one is without feeling of compassion, one is not human." (Mengzi 2A6; Van Norden 2008, 46)

Scientific research has studied and measured the biological electromagnetic waves of the physical reaction of the heart in relation to random flashcards showing positive and disturbing images. The vagus nerve connects the brain to the body's significant organs, including the heart, which allows us to sympathize with another person.

The biggest opponent in martial arts is the self, which is a reflection of our inner fears, anxiety, and emotional blockages. To overcome these, we see a parallel between the making of a samurai sword and the development of a warrior's inner strength. That strength is defined as *tanren*, or the forging of the spirit with the higher purpose of *budo*, meaning "the martial arts way." In building this, the student grinds against limitations in order to sharpen and polish his character.

Likewise, one's sword must be made carefully so that it remains powerful and firm in combat. A poorly made sword will break during battle, as will a warrior who's not patient or careful. The sword maker spends many hours making the samurai sword, known as *katana*. The process includes melting the steel and dissolving carbon into the steel, using high temperatures to remove impurities from the steel. There are two types of steel: high carbon and low carbon which are hammered and forged into the *katana*. The tough low carbon steel forms the inner core of the *katana* and the high carbon steel forms the outer part. The sword is then pulled from the fire and cooled by plunging it into water. The differences of the carbon result in the distinctive curvature of the *katana*. The blade is then polished, often taking up to two weeks, to create the razor-sharp edge. Grinding and polishing stones create the final product. The finishing touch is the decorated hand guard. It takes fifteen men nearly six months to create a single *katana*.

Just as there are no shortcuts in the making of the samurai sword, there are none in arriving at the martial arts way. This is not the only way, as I believe that many paths can incite passion and move the heart. When we find something worth living for, we're supported by a greater force that replenishes us in hard times. This idea, paradoxically, means we must accept who we are in our own development. The beginner must learn to accept defeat as a step toward personal growth. Dr. Kano's famous quote is, "It is not important to be better than someone else, but to be better than yesterday."

One of last samurai, Kaishu Katsu, who influenced Dr. Kano and Prof. Nitobe. Using the samurai mind for productivity.

Samurai believed their rigorous training and the Bushido code polished the self to achieve a clear purpose in both thought and action. If the heart-mind is pure, action is reflective of the inner self, as in a mirror or still water. One of the world's foremost martial artists, Bruce Lee, spoke of water during an interview in the early 1970's. Much of his philosophy had its origins in the ancient teachings of Sun Tzu, recognized as the author of the compilation of strategies known as *The Art of War.* Lee suggested that the inner self be formless:

> *"Empty your mind, be formless, shapeless—like water."*

> *"Now you put water into a cup, it becomes the cup. You put water into a bottle, it becomes the bottle. You put it in a teapot, it becomes the teapot."*

> *"Now water can flow or it can crash."*

The idea of fair play in combat-oriented competitions is evident in sportsmanship. In today's world, the Bushido concept allows each competitor to improve the other's skills, similar to iron sharpening iron. The Japanese word *shiai* means game or match. Originally, it meant someone's death. When samurai engaged in combat, one or the other would lose his life. In 1946, the concept evolved and *shiai* was redefined as "testing each other." As Carlos Gracie wrote, "There is no losing in Jiu Jitsu, you either win or you learn."

Another concept of collective cooperation is known as *ibukaiyu.* Its origin seems to be in ancient China and in an oral tradition stemming from Indian martial arts techniques brought to China 1500 years ago by Bodhidharma, the founder of Zen. He left India to pass on the teachings of Buddha, ending his journey in a Shaolin temple in the Henan province. The martial arts techniques he taught spread all over China. Ibukaiyu is a collaboration that allows for the mutual benefit of all who participate.

Beginning in 1958, Japanese schools brought some of these samurai concepts into the modern world, making ethics and morals part of the standard educational curriculum. This policy included an increased emphasis on the virtues of observing the law, respect for public property, love for family, and patriotism. The teaching of these values began for me in the second grade, when I took a class called *Doutoku*, meaning "The Way of Virtue." As I got older, this helped me understand the foundation of the Bushido code.

Since childhood, I'd admired Samurai culture because the samurai warrior was not only tough, but had wisdom—not school smarts, but practical intelligence. Some of them had gone to a different culture and challenged themselves in this way and that story inspired me as a child. They became my heroes. When I was in high school, I told my parents that I wanted to go to America and do martial arts. They were open minded enough not to say no, but they had one condition: acquire a bachelor's degree first. They had concerns for my future and often said, "Bunbu Ryodo" (be both a good warrior in the martial arts and a good scholar in school).

At university, I majored in International Relations Law and took some criminal law and business law. Some teachings were just theory, which bored me, but other professors explained with practical theory, which is what I was seeking. I boxed for four years in college as part of my Karate practice and was getting serious about martial arts training. I started to wonder, "What is the true meaning of strength?" which at that time was just a vague idea.

After graduating university, I didn't have enough money to come to America, but found a job as a bounty hunter. I saw it as a chance to use my martial arts and law knowledge. In pursuing the job, I was interviewed by two people, one a very tough-looking guy. They told me to go find a man who'd ordered a bunch of digital cameras and sold them to a third company, but didn't pay. The CEO of this company said whoever found the man first gets the job and the time limit was one week. The first guy I was competing with couldn't find him in a week and the second couldn't, either. I was patient and waited, catching him and turning him into the company. When he'd tried to fight back, I'd restrained him without hurting him. The CEO was very happy and wanted me to work for his company. But I declined his offer respectfully, received the bounty, and bought an airplane ticket to America.

Chapter 2

Bushido

武士道

*T*he ultimate goal of Bushido is establishing peace. The Chinese character, *BU*, means "stopping the sword." The world is not perfect and we must find practical ways to resolve conflict. Sometimes, this means fighting for something we love so that darkness doesn't take over. The founder of shorinji kempo, Sou Doshin, said, "Justice without strength is powerless. Strength without justice is violence."

As one consciously chooses to confront obstacles in life, rather than avoiding them, one must accept the challenge with calmness and tranquility of mind—with both the harmony of Bushido and the patience of the samurai. Patience is far more than waiting; it is remaining resolute and calm when one's expectations are delayed. If the inner warrior is following the wrong path, this will come out in his movements during training and combat. In my Karate apprenticeship, I was taught that how you train and how you fight is who you are. If a person is emotional, they fight with emotion. If the person is calm, they fight with calmness. The samurai sword in the hand of a warrior should reflect a high level of virtue.

All my martial arts mentors were warrior figures: meaning no talking, just doing. They taught me the way by learning through action. I wasn't the best student and classes were very hard physically and mentally, but they knew how to push me to the edge and break through my previous limitations. People often say that you will have a deeper understanding of things when you become a parent and martial arts instruction is the same way; now I grasp why the training was so difficult. It is endlessly challenging in order to make our spirit much stronger: a lifetime benefit.

Over and over again, I ask myself, "*What is Bushido in this particular situation?*" and I return to Dr.Kano's concept of using fortitude, dedication, and discipline in everyday life, not just in combat. I seek to instruct this way to my students and how the martial arts journey reflects a patient, long-term commitment to growth. This comes from knowledge gained slowly through the repetition of physical lessons. At the age of six, I began my journey by being constantly pushed to a cold and hard wooden floor by my instructors, who were Japanese riot police officers. This repetition of the training taught me patience and resolve. While it might not be the best way to teach in our modern culture, some things can only be taught face to face. However, with the internet and social media, we can now learn the Bushido way through more resources.

During training, my Kendo academy code required us all to say at the end of class, "Martial arts are your mindset. You must learn the mindset before you learn martial arts."

It took me awhile to learn the true meaning of this and how it could improve every part of my life. When I began training, I was seeking strength, but I was young and didn't know what true strength was. I remember that one of my school teachers told my parents, "Nobu only works hard at what he's interested in." I got in trouble for this, until I made a commitment to work hard at everything and continually challenge myself to grow. That in turn gave me the inner strength to come to America after university.

Once in the U.S., my commitment deepened, as I did full-time training. My Karate master was known as a living samurai in the full-contact Karate community. I worked with him six days a week, three times a day for two years. The lifestyle was very challenging, but the discipline I'd forged in my mind and body through following the Bushido code took me to the next level.

Chapter 3

Rectitude / Justice

義

*W*ithout the correct mindset, martial arts are just a weapon. With the correct mindset, they're a strong set of tools, especially for the young. Why the young? Because they're the future and kids have minds like sponges. Their thoughts and patterns of behavior become their reality, for better or worse. I teach them a five-step mindset and how understanding words and their meanings are keys to building good patterns for the self and how that relates to others. The training includes:

1. The ability to know when to say "yes" or "no." When faced with a challenge, this is the first decision for positive growth and avoiding negative influences. Do you have the right mindset and can you take action from there?

2. The understanding of the "Thank You"—a mindset of appreciation, not just as a preprogrammed response, but coming from deep gratitude.

3. Having empathy toward others when your actions negatively affect them, along with transforming errors and mistakes into positive outlooks with authenticity. For instance, when a child harms another child, encourage the first child to look at the hurt child's face and find the correct words to say. Just saying "Sorry" often doesn't allow them to feel how their actions have affected another person. Find the right words that show empathy.

4. How to use the term "I will"—the mindset of improving the self by creating responsibility. When you say "I will," commit to following through with your actions, no matter the challenges.

5. How to say "Thanks to you"—the mindset of humility and the realization that we grow both from the given circumstances and another person's influence.

Learning this mindset is the most important part of mastering the technical skills. In training, those skills can grow, but if we don't know how to behave, we can easily slide out of control and be harmful. In *Star Wars*, they call this process "going to the dark side of the force." This dark side is self-centered and has historically proven to be dangerous and unstable. Having a proper mindset is like a good base that evenly distributes weight and force throughout the entire structure; all parts work together in harmony for a greater purpose.

Natural basic stance of Judo. (Dr.Kano)
© Kodokan Judo Institute

"Rectitude" is the concept of choosing the road less traveled, a way usually more challenging. The origin of the word is from the Latin *rectus*, which means both right and straight. It's essential to understand not just rectitude, but also duty and obligation. In Japanese this is known as *giri* and *gi*. *Giri* is associated with social correctness and doing what is right; *Gi* is associated more with doing what is right within the context of justice.

The power of the Bushido code was that the concepts of right and wrong were not written down so it was up to people to understand their circumstances and adopt a feeling of mutual benefit. When something is codified in words, this can limit the choices of those who follow it exactly. One must be able to think for oneself in every situation. Knowledge can be just grasping theoretically what to do; wisdom is applying that knowledge properly. One way to approach rectitude is through understanding its application in *jita kyoei* (universal prosperity for earth, meaning for humans, animals, the environment, other planets, and all sentient beings).

Shikanosuke Yamanaka, known as a "challenge spirits samurai warrior," was famous for embracing hardships in order to polish his warrior spirit, by saying to the world, "Please give me seven difficulties and eight sufferings." He knew that all obstacles and challenges made for growth and strength, as well as self-improvement. *Jita kyoei* is about self-improvement—to become a better version of oneself. You can help others more when you have a better version of yourself (*Seiryoku Zenyo.*)

Coming to the U.S. to pursue martial arts, I was emotionally tested because of the language barriers and wondered if I'd made the correct choice. Many times I felt disheartened, but thanks to the community and gifts my martial arts teachers gave me, I was able to accept and appreciate my decision.

In samurai culture or Japanese culture we don't talk about suffering—it's just "suck it up and do it." When I came to America, I immediately felt lost because I lacked communication skills. It was challenging just to order a sandwich and I was bewildered by an unfamiliar culture and rules, including what is right or wrong. I went through many conflicts based on misunderstanding. My friends explained to me about Wild West history and I had to learn to balance my old identity with learning a different culture. I kept returning to the questions: What is right or wrong? Another way to put it is: What do I allow and what do I not allow?

In 2016, I had an opportunity to think more deeply about this when I had conflict with an attorney over a legal document that he'd made. He said everything we were doing was legal, but something felt wrong and I started to think, "What would a samurai in the modern world do in this situation? What's the meaning of the Bushido code now? Is there a difference between what is legally wrong and morally wrong?"

The attorney explained to me that if a person did a crime, but was shown to be innocent in court, then he was, in fact, innocent. I thought, "No, he's not innocent. A samurai would go after the person and discipline him." But I didn't say this to him or say it publicly. I managed this quietly and removed myself from the circumstances without creating more conflict. This incident was one thing that started me thinking about writing this book and examining the modern samurai way. I began broadening my education by reading about others who'd created the martial arts.

I learned about *Sensei* Mitsuyo Maeda's life story though the practice of Brazilian Jiu Jitsu. I was curious about his efficient art and dynamic spirit, which were like a modern samurai's. I found out more about him when Kodokan *Sensei* Murata taught me Dr. Kano's three-phase method at Kodokan, Japan. I saw how Mitsuyo Maeda had lived and followed this method. I used his experience to help myself after I came to America and needed a different set of skills beyond fighting.

Initially in practicing martial arts, I was just seeking toughness and effectiveness in combat. I thought I knew everything I needed to know from Karate, but I was wrong. In my twenties, during a challenge match using full-contact Karate, I was lucky to win by a knock out. I realized that I needed to learn from this, which was the start of my journey into Jiu Jitsu. There was more to fighting than toughness. I had to be smart as well and be able to adapt. When I came to America, I had to adapt and grow faster than ever. I had to use what I'd learned in the martial arts to be open-minded and flexible.

Again, I turned to someone who'd come before me. Conde Koma, aka Mitsuyo Maeda, was number one at Kodokan, according to Judo legend Kyuzo Mifune. People attribute Judo "theory and structure to Dr. Kano and its action by Mifune." *Sensei* Mifune was promoted to the tenth degree Kodokan Black belt. Dr. Kano believed if people exceeded their limitations, they could go even further (to the eleventh or twelfth degree), but right now tenth degree is the highest in Judo. When he joined the Kodokan, *Sensei* Maeda threw *Sensei* Mifune more than anyone ever had. Small in stature (5' 4" and 148 lbs.), *Sensei* Maeda used all of his skills, physical and mental, to dominate his opponent, his confidence on display on and off the mat.

Dr. Kano saw enormous potential in *Sensei* Maeda and sent him to Cuba to spread Judo theory and philosophy. Many people at the Kodokan were concerned that it would suffer without Maeda, but Dr. Kano believed in his decision (following this path, I later made my own commitment to come to America and share the martial arts).

In Japan, the rule was that there were no challenge matches for prize money, but in Cuba *Sensei* Maeda needed to make a living and decided to "break the rules." Japanese culture respects traditions and following customs, but living in the U.S. I've also seen the importance of practicality. In America, there's less tendency to judge what is good or bad. *Sensei* Maeda chose to change the rules in order to spread Judo and make a living. He was practical when it was necessary and treated people from various cultures from within the Bushido code.

After settling in the Amazon, he offered his land to the Kodokan for future practitioners. At the Kodokan, 100 years after Dr. Kano passed away one sees large pictures of *Sensei* Maeda on the walls. Dr. Kano promoted *Sensei* Maeda to 7th degree Kodokan Black belt for his contribution and his name is still prominent at Kodokan. A Brazilian Navy commander created a memorial statement regarding *Sensei* Maeda's outstanding martial arts contributions, integrity, character, and strong beliefs in the future. An ideal martial artist, his loss was greatly felt in the Amazon. He had to leave Japan and break the rules to move martial arts forward.

His academy (Academia de Code Koma) no longer exists and his successor was not directly established. Luckily, the Gracie family and other family members kept the art sharpened and evolving and were able to share it widely. It is important to see the big picture when evaluating right and wrong.

When faced with a decision leading to personal gain at the expense of others, one has an obligation to have a higher call to action. For the samurai, knowing what to do and doing it without hesitation led to a more cultivated and powerful expression beyond one's sense of self. Dr. Jigoro Kano encouraged us to have a big vision when considering right and wrong in relation to *jita kyoei* (mutual prosperity to self and other). We must sift through what we hold as true and evaluate where it may come into conflict with others. Dr. Kano saw mutual prosperity during the Westernization of Japan in the pivotal *Meiji* restoration (when samurai feudalism came to end).

Commodore Perry and his party landing at Yokohama to meet the Shogun's Commissioners.
By Peter Bernhard Wilhelm Heine, 1855, lithograph.

For centuries, during the time of the samurai, Japan chose to isolate itself from outside influence. The beautiful aspects of Japanese culture flourished in the arts, food, and a general mentality known as *kaizen*. This was a highly specialized way of living in higher purpose. When the black ships of Commodore Perry arrived from America in 1853, it threatened the entire country. The question of whether Japan should open its doors or fight to isolate itself divided the nation. A special samurai force was created to maintain the identity and security of what the world now treasures about Japanese culture.

As we see from history, right and wrong must take into account what is unchanging and benefits all in the long run. One truth of all cultures and religions is the value of love. As Rumi, the Persian mystic and poet, said, "Your task is not to seek for love, but merely to seek and find all the barriers within yourself that you have built against it." As the heart guides us beyond those barriers, we must operate from this unified field of connection to self and other.

With each breath we take, we're that much closer to our last one. It is truly powerful to live each breath, each step in the journey with a greater purpose. The word *dojo* means "place of the way," and if we consider our life experiences, we get to choose our responses to challenging circumstances versus the lower-minded tendencies of reaction. We must also be practical when considering right and wrong in terms of *jita kyoei* (mutual prosperity to self and other). For instance, if something could benefit everyone without draining resources, but potentially could also threaten humanity in the wrong hands, is it right to release it to the general public? Who's using the tool is of great importance and why teaching young people to think critically so is an important concern.

When we teach the younger generation in the practicality of martial arts, we have a responsibility to show them to keep going forward in a positive direction. At the end of class, their effort is rewarded for choosing to continue versus giving up. The next generation will have a solid mindset for facing challenging circumstances, but first comes knowing right from wrong and, ultimately, choosing rectitude.

Chapter 4

Courage: The Spirit of Daring

勇

*W*hen the samurai knows the difference between right and wrong, he can exercise virtue by choosing the former, which will help him face difficulty with bravery. It's essential for someone to understand his own capabilities before trying to help others. If someone is drowning and you don't know how to swim, you may cause more harm to yourself and that person if you attempt to save him.

One great aspect of martial arts is understanding fear and where it comes from, which is usually from the unknown. Our biggest fear is not physical death because we know it will come, but fear of our daily existence. Growth, by its nature, is uncomfortable because what once served an older version of oneself must die in order for a new version to be born. As we let go of what no longer works and learn how to relax in the face of conflict, we shine more light toward the unknown and carve out a new path. Courage comes with understanding our fears and applying this wisdom to face them in a constructive way.

I look back now with gratitude on my decision, in my early twenties, to leave Japan with one backpack and follow my dream to explore martial arts as a way of life. Crossing the Pacific Ocean meant facing a lot of uncertainty, as I left behind the comfort of my native language, culture, family and friends. My courage to do this has helped me help others who want to navigate the deeper parts of life. I'm grateful to everyone who helped me through the unknown and have no regrets about following my heart.

I believe that courage must have at its roots in benevolence and understanding oneself. Jumping into a deep, wild ocean with no awareness of how to swim is not courageous, but foolish. True courage is applying the correct knowledge to an action that helps self and others. With that courage we can recognize older versions of our own self in others and help that person instead of fighting them. I'm appreciative of the courage martial arts gave me to evaluate what version of myself didn't serve me anymore in America. It was challenging to let go of ways that inevitably created more conflict, but this gave me greater perspective to understand myself and others.

When I first arrived in the United States, I had several jobs: personal trainer at a 24-hour fitness club, sushi chef, working in a reptile store, a police supply store, the music industry as security at concerts, and as a bouncer. These various jobs presented many challenges because of language, rules, systems, and so many other unknown things. When I was seeking a practical martial arts job, a friend told me about becoming a bouncer at a club (because the previous bouncer had gotten shot). It paid well, but I took some serious risks with danger: one night a guy aggressively harassed a lady customer and was getting violent and the club owner wanted me to handle it. I used a Jiu Jitsu hold on the man without hurting him and made him leave the club.

At 2 a.m., the club closed and I went out to the parking lot. The guy was waiting outside and as I came toward him, he pointed his finger at me and said, "Bang!!!" as if he were holding a gun. He said he could shoot me so I had better watch out. I got chills, realizing that I really could get shot. I restrained myself and just said, "Thank you" and walked away. It was an unforgettable lesson about never becoming overconfident about one's skills—a life lesson in understanding that a samurai spirit can't conquer a gun.

Another time I needed to catch a gangster who'd stolen firearms from my friend's police supply store. My friend and I went after him and I took him down and sat on his stomach, a Jiu Jitsu position. My jeans got torn and my knee was bleeding. My friend pepper sprayed the man's eyes, but the wind blew the spray into my face and this burned my eyes and throat. I had to use all of my power and self-control to hold him down. Police officers came and arrested him and a crowd gathered around us on the street. My loaded gun, which I had to use in this type of security work, had fallen out of my jeans during the takedown. It was sitting out in the open, but luckily no one saw this and I retrieved it. From then on, a police sergeant I worked with back then called me Kato, from the *Green Hornet* TV show because I was working this type of job with no emotions; I just did what I had to do. And, I didn't speak much at that time because my language skills were lacking and I was still figuring out the communication systems in the United States.

I look back now and think about this experience and others like it. As a younger version of myself, I struggled to survive in a foreign country and there was no room to think about fear or risk in a deeper sense. I am now fortunate to be able to share these stories and life lessons on the danger of weapons and violence. It reminds me of the story I read about an ancient Chinese martial artist. Back then, the transport industry had to use horses as well as walking. The transport industry hired bodyguards who were experts in the Chinese martial art of Kung Fu to prevent assault by bandits. One martial artist, who was very good at what he did, was taking a rest with the transportation group in the city. Here, he was challenged to a match by another Kung Fu master. The transportation bodyguard lost this match and broke his spine. After that, he had difficulty standing up his whole life but he never stopped his training. He continued to teach so many great students and emphasized the concept "refrain reckless courage" from Confucius. And Confucius explained that "bravery without a sense of rightness at the sight of profit or taking no action when justice demands it cannot called real courage."

The Kung Fu master who broke the body guard's spine had a similar instance of being challenged to a match. But, in his case, he lost his life.

These brutal stories teach us how our mindsets influence behavioral choices which then influence our actions and circumstances.

> *Watch your thought;*
> *They become words.*
> *Watch your words;*
> *They become actions.*
> *Watch your actions.*
> *They become habits.*
> *Watch your habits;*
> *They become character,*
> *Watch your character.*
> *It becomes your destiny.*
>
> —Lao Tzu

When we practice martial arts, we are reminded of the virtues of appreciation, respect and humbleness in order to gain both inner strength and physical strength. The meaning of courage can be expressed in many different ways. We all face challenges and obstacles in everyday life; to display true inner strength, courage comes not from avoiding the obstacles, but rather in taking action to improve from these challenges. Even it it's just one inch of improvement, it's still something. To eventually break through obstacles, one requires this true inner strength through courage. When teaching kids martial arts, I realize the profound importance of giving them the tools to work through these experiences for the rest of their lives.

Chapter 5

Benevolence

仁

Without courage, you can't practice any other virtue consistently.
You can practice any virtue erratically, but nothing consistently
without courage...People will never forget how you made them feel.
—Maya Angelou, American poet, civil rights activist

There's a template that must be followed as we learn. In traditional martial arts, this is called *kata* (form). If we think of wood carving, form is like a square block. With training, the teacher encourages the student to transform the wooden blocks' rigid edges into a ball, which can then go anywhere while maintaining its form and function. Once the basic form is understood, one can use it to find one's own expression, even if it's different from others. What often undermines benevolence is forcing others' behaviors to meet our expectations. True benevolence challenges us to find constructive methods to bridge gaps in communication and misunderstanding. This requires a big heart and the ability to see one's self in others.

The philosophy expressed by Professor Nitobe in his Bushido book describes the virtue of benevolence as, "The bravest are the tenderest, the loving are the daring." Just as one bucket of water can extinguish a room on fire, benevolence can win over the spirits of others. Courage is allowing the inner self to thrive, while expressing the calm gentleness of benevolence. Both Confucious and Mencius acknowledged that the highest requirement for a ruler is benevolence. Shakespeare thought it more important than a king's crown. This concept is essential for any successful organization or community. If those with more experience use their power unproductively toward those with less experience, learning stops and growth is limited. Showing compassion to someone with less skill helps everyone.

Professor Nitobe's true intent was to make our world more peaceful, even though he was writing about samurai who were combat specialists. Samurai were meant to serve and to adhere to a higher ethic, a higher ideal. Without that, they were merely barbarians, like the beasts in the wild who lived only to survive. Humans, on the other hand, could learn from their history and nourish one another. While perfection is sought, benevolence is the quality that gently serves to offer correction.

When Professor Nitobe served in the League of Nations, the forerunner of the United Nations, he was instrumental in adapting the Bushido mindset to avert potential armed conflict and subsequent bloodshed between Finland and Sweden. He resolved an issue involving a dispute over Aland Island that resulted in complete disarmament. He showed that the Bushido code can be used for peace; for the exact opposite of combat. This embodied the concept of *jita kyoei*.

Sweep from guard position at kids' class.

Jita kyoei, or mutual prosperity, represents a greater cultivation of the mind and spirit over materialistic success. If your training mates are supportive and challenging, you might win sometimes and lose other times, but it's the best environment for growth. In kids' classes, I teach the principle of helping each other to grow physically, mentally, and emotionally. Just as humans can't live alone, we can't train alone for Jiu Jitsu. When the younger generation learns the importance of community, they'll create a better version of that community in the future. Martials arts can be part of that by training peaceful warriors. The more I do this work, the more I follow in the footsteps of my predecessors and heroes.

Professor Nitobe had high regard and respect for Kaisyu Kathu (1823-1899), an accomplished negotiator who helped in the transition of power during the Meiji Restoration from the Samurai Shogunate to the new

Meiji government. Kaisyu was a master swordsman who adhered to a strong belief in peace. That belief helped deliver Japan from the despotism of military conflict. Kaisyu never used his sword during the samurai revolutionary times, but only his "sword mind."

Another historical feudal samurai, Masamune Date, believed in balancing rectitude with benevolence. Too much rectitude made the warrior too firm, too brittle, and easily broken. An overabundance of benevolence led to too much softness; the person becomes a doormat. I see stubborn fighters who are stuck in a life pattern, locked in an old system with no room to grow. They just repeat the same things without evolving. Yet if a person is too soft, someone will take advantage of him. We have to find a balance between these two. Neanderthals had a strong physique and skills to use tools, but Homo sapiens became far more prosperous. In martial arts, flexibility is the key, just as in life.

By practicing benevolence and learning history, we can apply the modern warrior code to the multi-cultural challenges of our contemporary time, while we search for future peace. Professor Nitobe served as a bridge to the Western world and America from the samurai code of Japan. Today, we need to implement the same kind of evolution.

Sometimes, benevolence doesn't enable people to grow productively. Then, it is better to offer rectitude so we don't waste each other's time. Stern words can be shared, but when they come from the heart, this is felt with more impact and love. Oftentimes, the person receiving those words will grow more than when we choose to enable bad behavior.

Benevolence requires us to accept where we are and where others are as well. As we understand our own weakness through hard training, we become more sensitive to others' pain and suffering. As a teacher, the challenge is often finding the correct way to a student's individual fate of realization. Once there, the student will feel compelled and encouraged to go through it. When a student goes in a direction that's not efficient, forcing them is not *seiryoku zenyo* (maximum efficiency of energy for them and one's self).

In Japan, there is the traditional story from the terrible battle of Suma-no-Ura in 1184, when a prevailing warrior had his foe on the ground. Etiquette required that the winner determine whom he was about to dispatch, by looking at his face. When the triumphant warrior ripped the helmet from his victim, he saw a juvenile fighter. The surprised combatant, in a true representation of benevolence and mercy, helped the youth to his feet and implored him, "Off, young prince, to your mother's side." The young warrior refused to go, begging the winner to honor both of them by dispatching him on the spot. Professor Nitobe wrote of this incident, "In an instant the sword flashes in the air, and when it falls it is red with adolescent blood."

After the battle, the warrior, instead of celebrating victory, chose to renounce his samurai career. He shaved his head, put on priestly clothing, and spent the remainder of his days in a pilgrimage of charity and kindness, enacting the manifestation of benevolence. The point of the story from the original Bushido text is to learn from history and polish our character.

According to Professor Nitobe, "Often times...a marching soldier might be seen to halt, take his writing utensils from his belt, and compose an ode—and such papers were found afterward in the helmets or their breast-plates, when these were removed from their lifeless wearers."

In ancient Greece as well as in the Satsuma clan, the gentle and tender side of a warrior's spirit was encouraged. For Greeks, it was the study of music, while among the samurai it was the composing of verse and music. Young Japanese warriors were asked to listen to the sounds of the Uguisu (Warbler) and to write poetically of nature's music. Eventually, the music of the young samurai soul would awaken to the sweet notes of the Uguisu and the warrior wrote:

> *Stands the warrior, mailed and strong,*
> *To hear the uguisu's song,*
> *Warbled sweet the trees among.*

Looking back now, I realize how much benevolence has come my way from friends, students, clients, teachers, and, of course, my family. Living in a different culture, I made mistakes, but I learned from them. Friends in America helped me understand true compassion and benevolence, and expected nothing in return. They helped me grow. Their open mindset allowed for that evolution.

My Jiu Jitsu community in America has attracted many different types of professions, cultures, and beliefs. My own academy has people from lots of medical industries and several doctors. In class, the physicians sometimes ask to excuse themselves to leave because of an emergency call. They sacrifice their private time to serve others and in this we can see the actions of the warrior. The life-warrior mindset is about benevolence with one's mission, no matter what it is. I greatly admire the organization Doctors Without Borders—their mission, without any military training, is to go abroad to very dangerous areas and offer medical service, a highly worthy endeavor. (I will donate ten percent of the profits from this book to Doctors Without Borders.)

Modern life requires learning these lessons as a way of working toward the best version of one's self. The cultivation of tender feelings breeds regard for the value and suffering of others. Modesty and compliance, activated by respect for others' feelings, is at the root of the next principle: politeness.

Chapter 6

Politeness

礼

The end of all etiquette is to cultivate your mind.
—Inazo Nitobe, *Bushido*

*I*n Jiu Jitsu, we bow before and after the match, whether we win or lose. A feeling of appreciation comes from a genuine bow, which lends itself to being open to new experiences and new lessons. As you honor your opponent, you embrace all he may throw at you as something to learn from, versus our natural reactive tendency. As Carlos Gracie said: "… in Jiu Jitsu there is no winning or losing, only learning." Even in losing, you make a future investment in your martial arts education. When you bow, you expose the vital parts of your neck and demonstrate your faith in the training.

Humility is felt when you bow from the heart. A Japanese interpretation of this act is, "When a rice plant comes to fruition, its head touches the ground." As we become stronger, we're encouraged to use that strength to nourish those around us rather than to push them down. As the student warrior, we gradually learn to control our physical power with our inner strength. The seeming paradox is that no one learns martial arts to be weak. With the strength attained through years of training, one learns how truly precious life is.

Politeness is a sense of calmness also found in sports and any other human interaction. I had the honor of training professional hockey players Jerome Iginla (six-time NHL All-Star and two-time Olympic gold medal winner) and Joe Colborne (1st round draft pick), in the art of Jiu Jitsu. I was impressed and inspired by their calmness and politeness and good manners.

I remember when Jerome first arrived at the front desk for information about private lessons. He was very nice and I felt something strong inside of him (he had enough confidence not to act tough.) I didn't know who he was, but after our initial session, I was amazed by his focus and skill and physical fitness. He was respectful and humble. I asked him, "What is your profession?"

"I play hockey professionally," he said.

At that time, he was with the Colorado Avalanche.

Then I understood why his athletic skills, core stability, and muscle endurance were above those of normal people. It opened my mind to the idea that sports offer people so many potential benefits—if they have the correct mindset. Sometimes, we see or hear that pro athletes act cocky or have unethical behavior. Power, money, and fame can take you to the dark side, but Jerome was strong enough that these things didn't affect him. One of my students explained Jerome's achievements to me and my appreciation of him grew. He showed respect for my school and was very down to earth. Another student from Canada told me that he was a super star in his country, a legend in the NHL.

As I taught him Jiu Jitsu, I was learning how he focused and was always seeking a new challenge, like a true warrior. He introduced me to one of his teammates and we started to train together as well. Jerome was a great role model for kids, a hero to them, the way we hope our sports stars will be.

If we disregard manners, it creates conflict and evolution becomes more challenging. While every culture has its own expression of etiquette, we're all encouraged to recognize the sincere expression of the heart.

Humans differ from animals in that the latter are naturally suited for combat. They don't need martial arts because they know how to move and act as a predator or prey. As people, when something flies at our face, we usually close our eyes and make our bodies stiff so we won't be hurt. In martial arts, we're trained to keep our eyes open and to move our heads or dodge the object. We learn to make these unnatural movements natural.

In the same way, when confronting emotional stress, we need to find our inner strength, instead of panicking or trying to avoid the situation. This is the path of the true life warrior—to evolve from the natural reaction (animal instinct) to consciously choosing a (human) response.

The days of using chokeholds in the martial arts to kill an opponent are long past and we can now use this training with a deeper sense of humility and acceptance. The person you're fighting is not a mortal enemy, but a decent human being who will neither kill you nor unnecessarily cause injury. As the warrior becomes stronger, he gains a greater awareness of the value of life.

According to American zoologist Dean Bashford, when speaking of the six elements of humanity, politeness is elevated to an exalted position, an expression of higher awareness of the self and others. As we train in martial arts, we understand the true nature of conflict is not with another person but with the self. Our opponents are there to test our own skills, minds, and emotions. When you fight a weak opponent, you will be sure to win and that will not challenge you to grow. When you have a far better opponent, you will discover more of who you are. Dr. Kano's original idea was for Judo to be a test of one's self. Sports competitions are one of the great tools for self-growth.

The politeness we show our opponents is an expression of our gratitude and hearts' willingness to be open. If we can show good manners authentically in competition, our minds are more accepting to changing conditions and evolution. Again, this process is not natural, but requires training to bypass our fight-or-flight response.

If we hurt our training partners or create a hostile environment for them, we'll soon run out of partners. The goal is to create a community where anyone, regardless of status, can benefit. This develops a healthy relationship between the self and another. Dr. Kano held this concept, *jita kyoei*, as one of two foundational ideas of Kodokan Judo.

In martial arts, the tea ceremony is an example of bringing grace and politeness into one's life. Its primary goal is inner peace, as well as a clear feeling of emotion and quietness of manner. English philosopher Herbert Spencer defined grace as the most economical manner of motion. Ultimately, it becomes the art of cultivating calmness of mind.

To the novice, the art of the tea ceremony seems tedious, but there's a purpose to the manipulation of a tea bowl, the spoon and the napkin. While desire could take over and cause us to chug the tea in one sip, we learn how to cultivate our impulses into refined movements. Likewise, in the heat of combat we learn how to channel and control our actions so that we can respond to our opponent with the most efficiency. In the tea ceremony, we learn awareness of subtle movements and how to be authentic with yourself and your partner.

When engaging in the tea ceremony, the samurai put his sword aside before entering the tea room. In similar fashion, the modern martial artist seeks harmony with everyday life. A well-trained martial artist doesn't need to act tough, but can hold a calm and gentle demeanor that makes everyone around him feel at ease. This goes back to the origin of the bow and the rice plant. If we get power, we are responsible to use it to help others sincerely, not make them feel powerless.

Seimu Ogasawara, in speaking of etiquette and courtesy, said, "The end of all etiquette is to so cultivate your mind that even when you are quietly seated, not the roughest ruffian can dare make onset on your person."

It's important to understand the difference between empty rituals and truly acting polite. When we sincerely want to help someone, we embody the spirit of extending ourselves to the other person, just as the bow extends the neck forward. If we blindly go through the motions of being polite without fully connecting to the other, it's like learning a *kata* without knowing the application. The "one-eyed dragon," Masamune Date said, is the same as offering politeness with no intention and it is meaningless.

In martial arts, the practice of *mokusou* is a proper meditation to understand the quality of stillness. All movement comes from stillness and the ritual gives meaning to movement. Politeness is learning how to harmonize oneself with another person. As we embody politeness, we create less disturbance and gain greater awareness to assist others in need. *Mokusou* teaches us to be calm regardless of circumstances.

Working in America, I'm grateful to be able to share the art with different races, genders, cultures, and religions. The politeness I've received has been universal from every culture and region. I have many students whom I see as warriors with character, and who act with true politeness. One was an Air Force Master sergeant who came to me after he'd lost his confidence, his family, his money, and had hit bottom.

As we trained together, I saw that day by day he was gaining his strength and confidence, facing his emotional challenges and breaking through his other obstacles. He carried on with his military duty, while studying with me and helping teach kids in my classes. He was also earning a bachelor of human science degree and was soon winning Jiu Jitsu championship titles and getting a promotion in the Air Force. It was great to see him grow and accomplish all of this in just three short years.

From him, I learned that there are coachable students and others who have mind blocks. The coachable ones are the most humble and approach martial arts with true politeness. I love the good humor in the Jiu Jitsu community, such as: "Leave the ego at door with your shoes." (It is taboo to step on the mat with shoes in the martial arts community.) In martial arts, politeness is about keeping an open mind to be ready to learn under any circumstances. We use the ego to grow in efficient ways instead letting it hold us back in inefficient ways. To overcome oneself in our lives, one must overcome the negative influence of the ego. Politeness is the reflection of uprightness and sincerity in our behavior and mannerisms.

Chapter 7

Sincerity

誠

*T*he warrior's virtues are not singular lessons, but are incorporated and interconnected with each other. Sincerity is part of all that we've learned so far and all that we're about to learn. Politeness without sincerity is superficial, not real. According to Masamune, "Doing something without sincerity becomes a lie."

The *kanji* (Japanese letter) for sincerity is the combination of letters for "word" and "perfect." Sincerity is what you do, based on what you've said. Simply put, actions speak louder than words. In the samurai community, it's greatly important that one perform his tasks in a straight-forward manner. *Bushi no ichi gon* means "word of the samurai." These warriors upheld their contracts without a signed and sealed deed because a samurai's word was more meaningful than a written document.

Sincerity is the quality of being honest, true, and authentic. From ancient days Confucius said, "Hold faithfulness and sincerity as first principles." Mencius characterized it as, "Sincerity is the way to Heaven." Politeness demonstrates that all of our small actions reflect our feelings; sincerity is a strong urge to help humanity.

Many people come to martial arts for different reasons and it's important to understand one's intention. What attracts us to a certain environment or circumstance is not coincidental or by mistake. As we approach our true purpose with more clarity, our environment shifts and things change on the outside. Often we must reevaluate our position and not get stuck.

This is similar to Lao-Tzu's famous saying, "A journey of a thousand miles begins with a single step." His deeper philosophy is that the thousand-mile journey begins beneath one's feet, and can come from a belief in any faith.

While Professor Niobe married an American woman and absorbed the influence of a different culture, he wrote about samurai virtue from this broader perspective, wanting to share the universal principles he believed in. Kodokan Judo founder Jigoro Kano also studied the virtues of various cultures and blended them into his work on how physical education with the right mindset helped us grow to achieve maximum efficiency. He was following the earlier path of Kaishu Katsu. As the first Asian on the International Olympic Committee, Dr. Kano helped shape the modern Olympic format. He showed Bushido virtue to the world for peaceful purposes, without any specific religious affiliation.

I've also had to learn more about sincerity and clarity of purpose, especially after coming to America. In Japan, I had a lot of support, but in the U.S. I was challenged on every level. One of the hardest challenges was language. On certain occasions, inconsiderate people told me to speak English when I was speaking English. I'd studied English from middle school to university, but the classes were more about memorizing than speaking English to others. I made progress and took on more responsibility and could have gone backwards instead of forward. I was raising a child, but in some ways she was also raising me and helping me grow as a human being. It's the same with our environment or circumstances. We can choose to grow or not, depending on how we use self-control and discipline.

What is contemplated in the heart, the center of your being, is the beginning of action and your journey. Sincerity has its origin in the heart. A dramatic example of this came from the Shinsengumi, a special police force established in Japan from 1863-1869. It was comprised of both samurai and ronin (samurai without a master or clan) and it possessed great skill, using the samurai code to organize and maintain order within the group. All members were extremely obedient in following the samurai way. If they gave their word that something was to be done, the task was completed. They embodied sincerity.

During the transition from the old ways to the new Japanese era, exemplified by the Meiji government, the hereditary stipend of *karoku* (a salary of rice) was abolished. Prior to this, if a battle was to be fought, the samurai did the fighting. The new government broke down the samurai system and established a military using conscription. The Shinsengumi warriors struggled to make a living.

In samurai culture, they were not supposed to do business even when they needed to, but let monks or lower-ranking samurai handle this. They believed that money was dirty and they had no skills for running businesses. Frustrated by the new Japanese government, they didn't fit in to the modern world and needed more than toughness to survive. They needed to be educated in different ways for a different world.

After 1876, many samurai had to focus on this new mindset and make a living in the new business world of Japan. While the warrior mindset continued, it was a difficult adjustment because they lacked these practical skills. Some failed at first, but not all. A key person in this transition was Mituyo Maeda, aka Conde Koma, who taught the Gracie family in Brazil about Jiu Jitsu and Judo. The Gracie family was successful financially and when Conde Coma came to them as a samurai, he was not. The family promoted him and helped spread the message of martial arts around the world.

Today, my mentor Rigan Machado has trained actors Ashton Kutcher, Mel Gibson, Chuck Norris, Keanu Reeves, and more. Jiu Jitsu has become part of pop culture for the new generation, just as yoga has in America. Younger people in the U.S. know little about the philosophy behind the martial arts and that is part of my mission. Along with teaching practical skills, I want to share more about the foundations of warrior virtue. As a professional instructor in America, this is my focus: to spread the martial arts to other cultures, while keeping it rooted in the ancient principles. I want the younger generation to receive the full benefits of martial arts training, which is a combination of physical education and practical self-defense skills. The true benefit, for every generation, is gaining confidence while learning to be humble.

Kaisyu Katsu influenced Professor Niobe and Dr. Kano, who influenced Maeda, and Maeda influenced Carlos Gracie. I hope to carry on this tradition by sharing the art with those in the future.

When I came to America, I met so many people who have had financial success and are independent and very helpful to each other. I've found that money is not a good or bad thing in itself; it depends on how we use it. Mutual prosperity can be a win-win situation, and business people are good at finding practical solutions. I'm still learning the business of giving back to community. I'm trying to teach the value of living the samurai code and applying it productively to the mutual benefit of all.

The samurais' great skills were self-control and inner strength. They had to have self-control because they were allowed to carry swords. Someone with a short temper would not be given this weapon. Today, we have to have respect and understand that cooperation, combined with an ancient warrior's virtues (courage, benevolence, rectitude) is required for modern life. Humans are like nuclear energy. We can be used destructively or productively, but we need to place our energy in alignment with the Bushido code to create a more peaceful future.

As we live the code, it provides a sense of responsibility to serve one's positive growth and the greater collective. As President John F. Kennedy said during his inaugural speech in 1961, "Ask not what your country can do for you, but what you can do for your country." Martial arts training embodies the same idea. The tools and mindset given by your instructor are for you to uncover the greatest teacher within yourself. When in competition, or the battlefield of life, no one can fight for you. You may know what to do, but to act on this with sincerity is the profound quality of moving toward universal truth.

As humans we can say something harsh, but if it's done with sincerity, it moves the heart and can actually feel good to receive. For example, coaching requires one to say challenging things to a fighter or student, but it's only done for their development and growth. Martial arts training and combat sports competition are like lifting weights; the resistance is there to build more skills and more muscle. "Good medicine tastes bitter," is a Japanese proverb.

Sometimes, we don't say things because we don't want to be disliked, but saying them the right way can be a great benefit to students. In the same way, I see parents who don't want to discipline their kids because they're afraid they won't like them. This isn't true benevolence, but avoidance. Jiu Jitsu skills are displayed by belt color and to earn a black belt takes an average of ten to fifteen years. As business people, we sometimes make customers happy by just giving a belt as an appreciation, but if they're not skilled it's not a true belt. Giving away belts as a customer service to make more money waters down the art and isn't good for the art or the students.

I believe that we all must put meaning on the color of belt. It's challenging to educate those new to martial arts in the belt system and balance this with running a business and instructing in the art of Jiu Jitsu with sincerity. Some people want to see results too soon, as if they tried to eat foods before they were fully cooked.

Kodokan Belt ceremony.
© Kodokan Judo Institute

The warrior code is flexible and offers the sincerity needed to exist in harmonious and peaceful ways. I strive to help students make the necessary adjustments to discover the best version of themselves.

Chapter 8

Honor

名誉

*T*he word stands alone, nearly sacred, combining all the virtues of the warrior way and is at the very foundation of Bushido and a samurai's core beliefs. It is defined as treating others with respect, integrity, and fairness. Before you're capable of doing this, you must have the knowledge and ability to treat yourself in this manner. In modern times, I believe that honor has a strong connection to finding your life path and following it, regardless of the circumstances. An honorable action doesn't seek recognition, but aligns and confirms someone's purpose in life.

One gift of the information age is our great access to ancient wisdom. The pains and tremendous amount of time it took our ancestors to gain wisdom is now right at our fingertips, if we fully commit to using these resources. While samurai had a strong commitment to their purpose and played the game of life with a single intention, we're presented with far more ways to do this. When one thing doesn't work, we can hit the restart button. This can be an asset, but also a crutch that keeps us from ever reaching our goals. So we must define and refine our sense of honor and use warrior wisdom each day.

From the beginnings of samurai culture, honor was more valuable than wealth or a warrior's own life. To emphasize this, in 1946, martial arts redefined the word *shiai* to a new and evolved meaning: "testing each other." Previously, it was defined as "meeting your death." In earlier times, the terms *hara-kiri* and *seppuku* meant self-imposed ritual death, an integral part of the samurai code. When the warrior failed in his duty, taking his own life was the way to assume responsibility. The actual meaning of *seppuku* is the opening up of the stomach with a *tanto* sword (short blade). The belly is where they believed that their fighting willpower came from, in the yoga third chakra. The action was symbolic of their devotion to a purpose greater than life itself. On the battlefield, the preservation of honor meant to meet your death with no regrets. Today, I believe it means to learn lessons and build the best version of one's self in order to create a better life through challenges. In doing so, we honor our ancestors, our community, and ourselves by living with sincerity.

From the late 1870's through the 1880's, Dr. Jigoro Kano, who extensively studied Jiu Jitsu and eventually founded Judo, realized that samurai martial arts needed to be transformed from the *shiai* philosophy into a more progressive principle. Dr. Kano decided on the *gi* (the loose fitting, two-piece martial arts uniform) to be white because it represents an exalted color in Japanese culture, as seen in the country's flag.

In today's Jiu Jitsu environment, the *gi* can be more adaptable for the student wishing to wear white, blue or black colors. Students enjoy the fashionable element of their training, but are still committed to the warrior philosophy as each one evolves within his own framework. Dr. Kano organized and converted his teaching to be consistent with the samurai combat system and samurai culture, maintaining politeness, courage, and honor. He was open-minded in his creativity, adopting degree techniques that incorporate Japanese chess (*shogi*) and the game of Go.

*Samurai Ju Jitsu/ Jiu Jitsu (Tenjin-shinyou style / Kodokan Judo
was made from this style and Kitou style.*

© Kodokan Judo Institute.

He also encouraged *kata* and *randori* as methods of maintaining the core of martial arts as they evolved in more modern ways. *Kata* is a technique drill and *randori* is sparring. *Randori* is a safe way to test martial skills and grow from the experience rather than die on the battlefield.

The concepts of *kata* and of *randori* are similar to the idea of grammar and a sentence, as it's important to have both. Grammar is merely the template, but the sentence uses grammar creatively. *Kata* is, therefore, an important component, along with sparring. The idea of practicing both drills and sparring is the essence of learning, helping the body and mind to grow simultaneously. It's difficult to create self-defense situations, but sparring assists in applying learned techniques in different scenarios.

The ultimate aim of Karate lies not in victory or defeat,
but in the perfection of character of its participants.

—Gichin Funakoshi, Karate pioneer

The *randori* concept and Dr. Kano's philosophy of *do* (the way) also influenced Karate as well. Karate's pioneer, Gichin Funakoshi, admired the Kodokan and Dr.Kano's work. *Sensei* Funakoshi integrated the concepts of *randori* into the art of Karate and called it Karate-do. These concepts were also adapted by *Sensei* Mas Oyama, the pioneer of full contact Karate known for its power, practicality, and non-quitting spirit. While *Sensei* Funakoshi wasn't granted access to learn from Dr. Kano, he gave *Sensei* Funakoshi the honor of demonstrating Karate at Kodokan and he utilized the art to contribute and enhance lives in a productive way. The link between Judo and Karate-do is not expressly established, but the goal of both is to polish the character of the students. There is one *do*, but many ways to express it without losing its essence. This is how honor remains intact through changing times.

A well-known Russian combat art, Sambo, was founded by Vasily Sergevich, who learned Judo at the Kodokan from Dr. Kano. Vasily spread Judo in the Soviet Union around the 1930s, but couldn't practice it publicly under Joseph Stalin's rule.

In the past, honor was valued and held a do-or-die reality. Nowadays, we're inundated with so much information that it's hard to connect authentically to honor and commit to it. One can easily make dishonorable decisions for a short-term benefit, like a martial artist buying a belt and self-promoting himself to a higher rank. The more he does this, the more he runs the risk of being exposed as dishonorable and fraudulent.

Warrior training develops inner strength over a long period of time, patiently building the confidence that we can grow positively, regardless of the outcome of fighting an opponent. Likewise, a self-promoted black belt may feel less confident when facing a legitimate foe. Often times, martial arts practitioners become concerned about the belt and place too much value on it. They confuse this with honor; but we can't seek honor for honor's sake. When the instructor promotes a student, this carries a sense of responsibility that includes honor. With the black belt, this sense of honor encourages continual growth in a positive direction.

The central idea of *jita kyoei* is mutual benefit and we see many progressive companies utilize this as a strategy for long-term growth. While honor may not be the primary mission, companies that focus on ethical and environmental sustainability tend to be more honorable.

Honor exhibits different expressions depending on the times. A most instructive and influential time in Japan's history was the Edo period, also called the Tokugawa period. This era occurred from 1603 until 1868 under the Tokugawa shogunate, which held 300 regional daimyos (feudal lords). The Tokugawa period was established on March 24, 1603, by Tokugawa Ieyasu in Edo (now known as Tokyo). The period was characterized by economic growth, strict social order, an isolationist foreign policy, a stable population, no wars, and popular enjoyment of arts and culture. It ended with the Meiji Restoration on May 3, 1868, when Japan, under Emperor Meiji, emerged into the beginnings of modern Japanese culture, politics, and society.

During those periods of history, the honor that was prevalent remains a significant component in understanding the Japanese soul and spirit. The Bushido book, published in 1900, sought to recapture Japan's soul and become a model for helping bring a peaceful life to those who chose to experience a resurgence of the warrior way. I've adopted this model as my own.

Martial arts and Zen are of great benefit to all ages and a common influence from 400 years ago to modern Japanese warrior training (Kendo, Karate, Judo). An over-riding concept that prevailed during this time was evolutionary change, as demonstrated by Munemori Yagyu who focused on how samurai cultivated their abilities in times of peace. Many influences contributed to this transformation, including the skills Munemori perfected called Muto-Dori (controlling an enemy's sword with his empty hand). He possessed an open mind in adjusting martial arts for the new era and helped shape the modern way.

Another important samurai, Musashi Miyamoto, developed a two-sword style of combat, fighting 61 duels without a loss. His unique style (hyoho niten ichi ryu) was counter-intuitive to most swordsmen and highly sophisticated, focusing on the efficient use of motion and power. He had no excessive or unwanted movements, gaining maximum impact through subtle timing and staying far enough away from a swordsman to avoid immediate danger, while creating an opening to strike. An accomplished writer and artist, he utilized his philosophy to master both the martial skills and literary skills.

My goal is to teach the young to master martial arts and the mindset needed to attain a peaceful life. We must respect the history of the art, but apply it to present circumstances. As we do this, we can thrive and grow and learn to forgive ourselves and others. Mercy and forgiveness are the result of working toward a bigger purpose. When we notice ourselves or others going in the opposite direction, a course correction is a show of forgiveness. As humans, we tend to fear the growth that challenges our identity. When we face our fears and embrace the changes, we feel a sense of honor and goodness.

We have tendencies in our behavior, whether from DNA or life circumstances, which don't serve us well. But in order to grow out of them, we have to break free of our comfort zone and challenge our identity. Action with good intent will come back to us with good results for evolution, adding to our sense of honor.

A critical concept voiced by Dr. Kano is *seiryoku zenyo* or the idea of using minimum effort for maximum results. Efficiency of movement is the highest principle in martial arts learning. The ultimate goal is using your energy to achieve a high degree of power for the overall good of society. This furthers *jita kyoei* by fostering trust, respect, and appreciation of one another, to help each other improve. With a shared spirit of mutual prosperity, we can extend this concept beyond two people to society in general and finally to the world as a whole.

I traveled to Israel to conduct a seminar in Jiu Jitsu at an academy and the head instructor believed that martial arts helped develop the skills not just of civilians, but of those in the Israel military. I focused on martial arts as having both a sport aspect and a combat aspect, while discovering how living in a country at war affects the population. The standard Israeli greeting—*Shalom*, meaning peace—took on a far more dramatic meaning during my visit.

If we look at Japan's history during turbulence and wartime, very little was accomplished in terms of polishing one's character. Yet in times of relative calm and peace great advances were made in the technical aspects of samurai skill levels, as well as in human development and self-awareness. When the emphasis is on survival, artistry and mastering one's skills fall away. During a warring state period in Japan (1467-1603), a select number of legendary samurai emerged and ushered in unsurpassed peace, which greatly influenced modern Japanese martial arts even today.

One such master was Sekishusai Yagyu (1529-1606). In his later years, his smooth style of swordsmanship helped initiate the Edo period of peace that lasted until 1868. Sekishusai is credited with popularizing the bamboo practice sword used in Kendo. At that time, this "training device" resulted in a huge debate about its viability. Many samurai believed it dishonorable to accept a challenge with a bamboo sword; that was more like a game, because it was less likely to result in death. Eventually, samurai warriors learned how to use bamboo swords as training tools for higher learning and advancement in technique, which then evolved into a more refined fighting system on the battlefield. This change of perspective turned a dishonorable action into an honorable method of honing ones' skills.

Sekishusai's son, Munenori, demonstrated to shogun Ieyasu Tokugawa this technique, which impressed shogun Ieyasu because it represented a new way for the upcoming peaceful era. It signified not killing an enemy, but the concept of the Zen mind's influence on the sword and how the sword became a tool for how to live and develop self-awareness. The spirit of the samurai could live on honorably even in changing times and be transmitted to various cultures. Today we see the influence of calming the mind in martial arts, while incorporating meditation before and after class, regardless of religious affiliation.

Today, each individual who trains does so for his or her own reasons—for sport, fitness or self-defense. In my classes, the student is taught in a controlled environment, where the opponent isn't seeking to harm or exploit. However, if an event were to occur on the street, the student must possess the mindset of awareness and be able to notice even the smallest detail which might aid in defending oneself. When I was in Israel, it was an eye-opening experience to witness a calm mindset of readiness amidst everyday life. In unstable conditions, honorable actions are hidden like a sharpened sword, maintaining peace, but capable of striking when necessary.

One modern expression of honor was displayed in an MMA match between Rickson Gracie and Yuki Nakai, two martial arts legends known for their samurai spirit. Rickson is a well-respected Jiu Jitsu master from the Gracie family and a legend in the Jiu Jitsu community. In Japan, he's often described as the Brazilian samurai. *Sensei* Yuki Sakai is the pioneer of Brazilian Jiu Jitsu in Japan and a former MMA champion who practiced Nanatei Judo (a *newaza*-style) influenced from Kosen Judo. When I first decided to study Jiu Jitsu in Colorado, I called *Sensei* Nakai who gave me great direction on where to start.

During this one-day tournament, *Sensei* Nakai had lost his sight in one eye in an earlier match (VTJ '95). He kept this hidden from the public so it wouldn't tarnish the sport because he believed martial arts were important for people's minds, bodies, and confidence. Despite this loss of vision, *Sensei* Yuki Nakai kept fighting and advancing until the final match against Master Rickson, who recognized his opponent had lost his eyesight and chose not to damage *Sensei* Nakai's other eye.

Another example of honor came during a demonstration at West Point, the military academy in upstate New York. Maeda and Tomita, a wrestling champion, demonstrated a Judo *kata* and Tomita charged his opponent like a bull. Maeda grabbed both sleeves and performed a hip throw; when the wrestler stood, he was thrown again with a sweep. Then Maeda did *Tomoe-nage* (sitting underneath the opponent and putting the foot in the stomach area as the opponent launches overhead). Following this spectacular throw, *Sensei* Maeda went to *newaza* (ground techniques). The wrestler reversed him and Maeda tried to choke him, but the crowd didn't understand the concept of using chokes. Maeda transitioned to an armbar from the bottom, and the wrestler submitted in defeat. In Jiu Jitsu this position on your back is called the Guard. The crowd didn't think it was very special because of cultural and rule misconceptions. In wrestling, you can't touch your back to the mat (signaling defeat), but in Jiu Jitsu/Judo you could attempt a submission as Maeda did with the arm bar. While Maeda fought from his position with honor, the wrestler found it dishonorable to keep fighting him from his back.

Misunderstandings in expression, culture, body language, and perspective create division in the concept of honor. As we saw from the Maeda match at West Point, knowing the rules will help both sides learn and evolve their art. If the rules change, the winner and loser will change with them. Sometimes, we can't judge value from just results.

Two Warriors of Honor

1. Mitsuyo Maeda (also known as Conde Koma)

前田　光世

Four Kodokan warriors in Cuba.
Mitsuyo Maeda, aka Conde Koma (center, standing up).

© Kodokan Judo Institute.

Born November 18, 1878, in Funazawa Village, Hirosaki, Aomori Japan, Mitsuyo Maeda left an international legacy as an accomplished one-on-one combatant. He came of age during a dramatic period of revolutionary change in Japanese history, as the country transformed from the samurai era to a modern era. During his time, he may have been one of the toughest men on the planet, but he wasn't just a fierce competitor. He was also generous and possessed integrity, respect, loyalty, and honor. Born into a samurai family (he and his father were proponents of *Sumo*), Master

Maeda became a true samurai through his travels around the world. He's considered a bridge of Japanese Judo/Jiu Jitsu to Brazil, now a worldwide martial arts discipline.

At eighteen, Maeda moved to Tokyo and started practicing Judo at the Kodokan branch of Wasoeda University. The next year, he became a member of Kodokan. Mitsuyo Maeda's journey had a rough start, as he was involved in many street altercations in Tokyo, but he trained so proficiently at Kodokan that he was eventually appointed an instructor. Dr. Kano assigned Maeda to Tsunejiro Tomita, the smallest instructor at the school, illustrating that in Judo size is not important.

He received more instruction from Yoshitsugu Yamashita, who later gave President Theodore Roosevelt private lessons in the White House. Yamashita also taught Judo to Roosevelt's wife, as well as other interested wives, showing that those of smaller stature could contend with and defeat bigger and stronger opponents. One of his female students was the granddaughter of General Robert E. Lee of American civil war fame.

When Maeda, Tomita, and Yamashita traveled to America and conducted demonstration matches, little did they realize the eventual impact this would have for the spread of martial arts in western culture. While Maeda did not speak a high level of English, the two other instructors were quite effective in understanding the language. Nonetheless, there were many times that Maeda learned difficult lessons due to his lack of language skills.

During the demonstration challenge match at the United State Military Academy West Point, Maeda met an opponent who was awarded points because it appeared that Maeda had been pinned during a wrestling maneuver. Because he failed to comprehend the significance of this, Maeda kept grappling and submitted his opponent from his back (by armbar—hyperextending his opponent's elbow), unaware that those observing the match considered his continuing to fight poor sportsmanship. Following the match, Maeda concluded that despite the controversial finish, the samurai code compelled him to continue on the battlefield as a statement of honor.

After New York competitions where Master Maeda showed his prowess by winning two straight matches and then a third opponent chose not to fight him, Maeda had the opportunity to become the co-owner of a U.S. gym. Americans were not familiar with the detail-oriented martial arts discipline system, in which basic moves were repeated continuously. Because of this, Maeda encountered financial difficulties. An acquaintance advised him to earn income by engaging in challenge one-on-one matches, but Kodokan had strict rules against this. Nonetheless, Maeda began accepting more and more of these fights as his success grew. In the matches, Maeda displayed the effectiveness of his art and many people grew to respect his character, polished by samurai code.

One of his favorite sayings (and one of mine) is, "Slow is smooth. Smooth is fast."

2. Saigo Takamori

西郷　隆盛

Saigo Takamori was born January 23, 1828, in Kagoshima state, Japan, and became one of the most influential samurai ever. One of three great leaders during the Meiji Restoration, after the demise of the Edo Period, he was recognized as the last true samurai. His character was portrayed by Katsumoto, the samurai leader in the movie "The Last Samurai." Initially, he served as a low-ranking samurai official. He was part peasant and part warrior and despite receiving a stipend, his family was quite poor. It took Saigo 25 years to repay the family debts.

During the Meiji restoration, Japan was in the midst of opening its doors to western influence, after isolating itself for 300 years and there was much conflict about Japan's future. One group was against westernization and supported the emperor. Saigo Takamori initially supported the Tokugawa shogunate, but realized that it wasn't where the world was headed. In the end, Saigo became known as a person who supported all of humanity. Through his negotiating skills, he successfully avoided bloodshed and cared for his injured opponents by taking them back to their families.

Saigo perished on September 24, 1877, in the last samurai war for the future of Japan. He died honorably for a bigger vision for humanity and his actions in a time of challenge and hardship were a display of his sincerity. A small number of individuals in the history of mankind are truly ahead of their time. Saigo had extreme loyalty to a purpose greater than his physical existence and is one whom history remembers.

In my own journey in America, I've had the honor to meet so many people with great personalities and talent. I've had the opportunity to face world-level competitors who had the dedication and self-discipline to become who they are. I've learned that warriors now are anyone who tries to make the world a better place. I've expanded my own view of the samurai way and am honored to have met so many warriors in totally different areas of life.

Chapter 9

Loyalty

忠義

Keiten-Aijin (Loyal to Universe Principle, Love People)
—Saigo Takamori

Saigo Takamori was a great contributor to the Meiji restoration, when Japan had to create a new system and way of being. The old ways and the new were in conflict, resulting in much confusion. Saigo Takamori chose the side of *jita kyoei* (mutual prosperity) and commonly wrote this as *keiten aijin* (feeling indebted to the universe and love for people). Blind loyalty can be very dangerous, but throughout his life, Saigo Takamori was a good example of loyalty with a proper mindset.

Loyal is defined as being faithful to one's oath, commitment or obligation. An oath is a vow, a solemn promise by which a person is bound to act. Loyalty has a unique standing within the samurai warrior code. The warrior lives knowing that life is temporary, but honor and loyalty are eternal. The Japanese national anthem embraces the concept of timelessness "…the eternity that it takes for small pebbles to grow into a great rock that is swathed with moss."

As Bushido teaches, Japanese culture sees things in very long terms. In the warrior code, an individual accepts a higher ethic not just for the present, but throughout time. The virtues of honor and loyalty have over the centuries changed to include mutual prosperity for all. One result is the peace found within the refuge of the higher ideal. A beautiful phrase from Saigo Takamori says, "Respect heaven, love humans." A deeper look at this means doing what's right, following your heart, and not having blind loyalty.

In the time of the samurai, there were no written rules, but a very high standard of warrior virtue. What created order was how the samurai transferred their beliefs into how they lived. Whether one met defeat on the battlefield or had to live under bad leadership, the true test of loyalty resided within the warrior's heart and spirit.

When I was a child, my dad told me a story about loyalty within our family ancestry. My ancestors were on the losing side of a conflict and following such a defeat, the prevailing side offered some short-term gain to its opponent. My family chose to maintain loyalty to its clan, giving up our samurai rank and losing our name and the right to carry a samurai sword. This story provoked my interest and made me curious about samurai and their view on loyalty.

As I become an adult, I grasped that my ancestors had understood the impermanence of all things and were willing to change. Nothing stays the same and, after the defeat, they wanted to evolve and start their own *sake* business. It became a success and they chose a new name: Yagai, from Yagai castle. Hearing about this got me interested in ancient warrior stories and inspired me to follow the path I'm still on. There are better ways to live than by pursuing blind loyalty.

A similar example is found in the life of Conde Koma (Mitsuyo Maeda). A highly successful student in the Kodokan School, Maeda chose to follow a different path in the world arena of competition, where he attained great acclaim and success. His path was contradictory to the requirements imposed by Kodokan, but he wanted to promote martial arts beyond Japan. He offered his rights in Brazil to Dr. Kano out of concern for future of Kodokan. Dr. Kano was very appreciative of Maeda's effort to spread the art of Judo and Maeda is still listed in the history of Kodokan as a 7ᵗʰ degree black belt.

Another example of loyalty comes from Yukimura Sanada, a brave samurai who faced a losing battle, but stood by what he believed was right. His son, who wasn't yet an adult, wanted to die loyally by his father's side. Yukimura Sanada told him he didn't have to die and the son chose to live. This was 400 years ago, but it shows that even then some things were more important than loyalty.

In the modern era, I believe the challenge for loyalty is to lend our energy toward our own productive growth and the development of those around us. One person I worked with helped me grow in martial arts, but I couldn't handle how he lived. I chose not to be around him, which was difficult because he was my friend. Sometimes, we have to make very hard decisions about trusting others or trusting ourselves.

Dr. Kano instructing in Europe.
© Kodokan Judo Institute

Chapter 10

The Education and Training of a Samurai

It is great to train hard and become a champion,
but it is greater to become a good human being.

—Jean Jacques Machado

The transmission of knowledge is the art of education and it is important for the development of society. It depends on the source, the medium, and the receiver. Someone can have very good information, but if it isn't transmitted effectively, it's useless to the one who receives it.

At the Kodokan Judo institute, I was fortunate to meet with *Sensei* Naoki Murata, an author and teacher of Judo and of Dr. Kano's philosophy. He taught me the three levels of Judo, and that none was more important than the others, and that each balanced out the others. The levels are: *gedan* Judo (the foundational phase), *chudan* Judo (energy/emotional efficiency phase), and *jodan* Judo (transmitting the benefits to others and to society).

The essence of samurai training can be summed up in the term *bunbu-ryodo*—"the way of the pen and the sword." This means taking foundational theory and knowing how to put it in action when one's emotions are being tested. It's the ability to use that foundation in ever-changing circumstances and finding clarity. It was Dr. Kano who said *kata* (foundational form) is the alphabet/grammar and *randori* (testing the energy/emotional efficiency) is the composition.

When I was at Kodokan, I appreciated the advice I received from the former Japanese Olympic coach and educator of physical education of Judo, *Sensei* Motonari Samejima. He explained the importance of break fall (*ukemi*) in our development and taught me the connection between physicality and emotions in *randori* training when sparring. In the *gedan* phase, it's important to learn how to safely receive the ground when we fall and to know how to tap during a submission. This occurs when you're being dominated by a chokehold, or pressure to an artery or limb, and you tap on the ground to give up. If you don't, you might pass out or hurt your joints. It's like a knockout in boxing, but in Jiu Jitsu it's letting your opponent surrender without harm.

In the *chudan* phase, we learn how to get up and understand our mistakes, which brings emotional clarity. In the *jodan* phase, the inner strength we've gained helps us see the bigger picture in our development and how to help others grow. The *chudan* phase tests our emotions when we're in a bad position and teaches how to convert this into a positive one. In an interview about Jiu Jitsu brothers Rener and Ryron, Gracie spoke about "the passing of the guard" which is a metaphorical and actual way in which an accomplished practitioner accepts his impermanence. In the *jodan* phase, this gives greater direction and motivation to help the next generation.

The balance of pen and sword evolved from the Tokugawa Shogunate, where warriors pursued martial arts and literary skills with equal emphasis, helping the samurai adjust from a period of war to an era of peace. Historically, the samurai education curriculum was structured in the following manner:

Ken Jitsu (Swordmanship); *Ju-jitsu*; *Ba Jitsu* (Horsemanship); *Sou Jitsu* (The Art of the Spear); *Kyu Jitsu* (Japanese Archery); *Heihou* (Art of War); *Shodo* (Calligraphy); *Doutoku* (Moral Education); *Bungaku* (Literature); *Rekishi* (history).

Kumiuchi (Samurai hand to hand combat.)
© Kodokan Judo Institute.

The original Bushido book emphasized Shodo and Jiu Jitsu. The skill of calligraphy (*Shodo*) was also important because it was considered a display of the person's character and spirit. Before one puts brush to paper, the mind must be still and then when form enters the mind, clarity of movement arises. *Kata* (form) in traditional martial arts begins with the mind, then the eyes, and the body follows. To be able to practice under any circumstances with a calm mind is why martial artists train so hard. Quieting can be achieved with meditation, and can work even when someone tries to push us as we meditate. Form and function is what we know how to do, but the challenge is doing it under emotional stress.

Dr. Kano customized a brutal battlefield art to reflect the changing era in Japan, moving toward the cultivation of human character through physical education (*tai iku*). His Jiu Jitsu (art of softness) became Judo (way of softness) and adopted a competition and belt system that reflected his desire to test and polish one's character in a supportive environment. This softness is referring to the quality of water, as Lao Tzu said, "Water is soft thing. It can penetrate the mountains and earth." Just as water flows and adapts to its container; information must also adapt to the times for knowledge to be transmitted.

During my high school education, my mindset in martial arts was primarily concerned with being tough. At that time, a UFC (Ultimate Fighting Championship) occurred in Denver, Colorado, in 1993. The event had no gloves, no rules, no weight classes, and was the first of its kind in the world. Professor Royce Gracie stepped into the cage and defeated three opponents without scratching or damaging them whatsoever. This feat was all over the media in Japan and profoundly shifted the face of combative martial arts globally. I remember reading a martial arts magazine with an interview with grandmaster Helio Gracie (Royce's dad and teacher) who explained that the art came from a Japanese man to their family in Brazil. It wasn't until my research for this book that I made the connection from Kodokan to Conde Koma to the Gracie family.

I read a biography about Conde Koma, *The Undefeated Combatant, Mitsuyo Maeda*, by Norio Koyama. The book gave impressive details about Conde Koma's life and challenge matches. After I studied at the Kodokan, I appreciated more how Conde Koma was able to adapt Kodokan principles in foreign countries. This cosmopolitan view was very progressive for Japan and helped influence the Gracie family, who then raised the awareness of the art to influence a new group of people. The information from Mr. Koyama's book gave me insight into how his experiences fit my own understanding of the three layers of Judo, after *Sensei* Murata had taught me about it at Kodokan. Since 1997, I've been instructing kids in martial arts and the more I learned, the more I felt it could be dangerous. Reading about Conde Koma and studying *Sensei* Murata showed me that martial arts must be taught in the correct way and with virtue.

Gedan phase of Mitsuyo Maeda (Foundation phase)

Mitsuyo Maeda joined Kodokan at age 19. Maeda's father was a village *sumo* (Japanese wrestling) champion. Since his childhood, Maeda's father helped create his base foundation of strength, both physically and emotionally. Dr. Kano and his top students helped to refine and polish Maeda's mindset and techniques. Maeda learned the Judo *kata* as well during this period, which became the template that served him overseas in his challenge matches.

Chudan phase of Mitsuyo Maeda (Practicality phase and learning how to control inner strength and emotion)

Prior to his international travels, Mitsuyo Maeda received a gift of a samurai sword from the future Japanese Prime Minister, Tsuyoshi Inukai. This was a great honor and highly indicative of the reputation that Conde Koma had in Japan. Dr. Kano saw the potential for Maeda to showcase the effectiveness of Judo abroad. Maeda's accepting of this foreign challenge became the *chudan* phase. In his career, Mitsuyo Maeda had challenge matches and demonstrations in Cuba, Guatemala, San Salvador, Costa Rica, Peru, Chile, Honduras, Nicaragua, Ecuador, Bolivia, England, Belgium, Spain, and the U.S. He embraced a larger world view and found a way to educate the public about the roots of Kodokan Judo.

One of his challenge matches was against an American wrestler, John Piening, "The Butcher Boy," dubbed the world's strongest wrestler (active from 1900-1907). Piening was 5' 10" and weighed 264 lbs. Maeda was 5' 4½" and 154 lbs. Maeda won two consecutive matches against Piening, the second of which resulted in Piening sustaining a hyper-extended arm after Maeda used an arm bar hold to gain the advantage. When Piening continued the match, Maeda prevailed, fighting under the name Yamato (which means Japanese samurai spirit).

Maeda fought additional matches in America, including one against a Chinese Kung Fu in a frontier-era town. In his career, Maeda had approximately 2,000 matches around the world. In his *chudan* phase, Maeda definitely challenged himself physically (going against bigger opponents) and emotionally, often not knowing the circumstances into which he was entering.

At this time, Kodokan was against taking prize money for fighting or accepting challenge matches unless this deepened one's understanding of the art. Rules and tradition were highly valued and it was still taboo for the sword-less samurai to deal with money. In the West, when Conde Koma chose to earn an income in fighting events he adapted to make a living and deepen his studies of martial arts. He shared his understanding of the art to help others. While in Madrid, Spain, Maeda wanted to develop a new ring name, but had trouble dreaming one up. In Japanese, *Komaru* is defined as trouble, but he didn't like the sound of this. He shortened the name to Koma and a Spanish friend suggested the word Conde (count in Spanish). Hence, Conde Koma, which Maeda considered humorous.

Jodan phase of Mitsuyo Maeda (Giving back to the community)

Koma shared and expressed the samurai way throughout his international travels. He was an instructor for a police academy and the Brazilian Naval Academy. He opened Academia de Conde Koma and was fundamental to the development of Brazilian Jiu Jitsu, especially through his teachings of Carlos Gracie. He also contributed to the lives of Japanese immigrants in Brazil by helping them settle into a tract of Amazon rain forest that was set aside for them by the Brazilian government and taught Judo to them and their children. Wherever he went, his success inspired people to open gyms and clubs, expanding the martial arts community around the world. This happened in Mexico when he taught Jiu Jitsu/Judo seminars and participated in challenge matches. Mexico established an academy after Conde Koma's demonstration of the practicality of Judo. Yet he never forgot his Kodokan roots.

While in Brazil, I had the great experience of eating dinner with the Gracie family and with Master Rigan Machado. They shared a family story of Grandmaster Carlos Gracie who, as a wild and dynamic young boy, jumped into the Amazon River near a crocodile. He survived, but came out of this just wanting to be tough, with little regard for the other aspects of the samurai way. When Koma became his Judo/Jiu Jitsu mentor, Carlos respected and listened to him because he was the Amazon's number one warrior. Carlos also studied nutrition with him and spiritual growth. He learned from Conde Koma not just the martial arts, but how to live.

Before Koma came to help, Carlos's dad, Gastão Gracie, was very concerned for his child. The boy was fourteen when he began training with Conde Koma in Academia de Conde Koma and was his student for four years. Today, Grandmaster Carlos Gracie is well known for contributing new ways of being through Jiu Jitsu, including lifestyle and even diet.

> *Jiu jitsu is the art of transformation.*
> —Carlos Gracie Sr.

When Carlos Sr. enlisted his assistance, Conde Koma was already well established in Brazil. He'd won a tournament with a number of warriors from the Amazon and was teaching in the university, the police department, at a naval base, and instructing Brazil's political VIPs. His work was the essence of Bushido. As Dr. Kano's demonstrations had earlier impressed the governmental forces in Japan, Conde Koma did the same in Mexico, El Salvador, and Brazil. The presidents of these countries welcomed him and his art with open arms.

When Katsu Kaishu saw Dr. Kano's demonstration, he was also moved and saw the potential to move society forward. His famous phrase after attending the complete ceremony of *Shimo-Tomisaka* dojo in 1894 was, "With no disturbance in mind, feel the wonder of nature and without intentional action, pursue the essence of change."

Katsu Kaishu gave this calligraphy to Jigoro Kano with words of praising his character with virtue and his high martial arts skill.

© Kodokan Judo Institute.

Conde Koma was a generous and happy-go-lucky spirit. During his time as a warrior, focusing on the business aspect of martial arts was still not acceptable. But this was starting to change. The traditional formalities of how students presented their carefully-wrapped tuition fees dramatically shifted when the education system in Japan became more westernized. It was now inefficient to open and count meticulously-wrapped money and new ways had to be found.

Many stories arose of Conde Koma sharing his fortune with those around him. He returned the generosity he received from Carlos Gracie's father, Gastão Gracie, by teaching Carlos the art for four years. During Koma's travels in South America, a thief stole his bag holding prize money and jewelry, including a diamond, along with his newspaper articles from around the world. In his good-natured way, he spoke of this incident politely, saying only, "Mr. Thief stole my bag." His *chudan* level training allowed him to transform his anger into a more positive and creative outlook.

After his four years with Conde Koma, Carlos Sr. opened his own academy in Rio de Janeiro, Brazil. Conde Koma had advised him to have a lot of children, and Carlos Sr. did, and the art flourished in many of his family members. It was a powerful experience to be at dinner with Masters

Crolin Gracie, Rigan Machado, Renzo Gracie, Robson Gracie, and Crolin's daughter, Kyvia Gracie, and to witness so many different expressions of talent. The Gracie family spread the art in a unique way, helping it grow in awareness, self-defense, sport, health benefits, and financially.

At this time, Professor Nitobe's Bushido book was published, enlightening the world to the warrior way of the samurai. Because of his global travels and his individual matches, Conde Koma was influential in a variety of international cultures, as he too was evolving with the art. His favorite phrase to his students was about having a mindset for integrity and to always be open minded. Later in life, he utilized the strength he gained from the *gedan* and *jodan* levels to help immigrant settlers from Japan in Brazil's Amazon region. Likewise, Dr. Kano spent his final years making Judo an Olympic sport. Both men showed how the three phases of Judo can be used for maximum efficiency to help oneself and others.

The concept of *onkochishin* means an attempt to discover new things by studying the past. The challenge of education is to maintain the essence of lessons learned and adapt them when times change. It takes a critical eye to evaluate what works and what doesn't. Unlike with samurai from the past, contemporary skills like mathematics, bookkeeping, and understanding money issues are all a part of the warrior's ethics. The Bushido code now relies upon gained wisdom and applying it to changing circumstances. As society evolves to greater levels of awareness and knowledge, the use of softness to influence a situation becomes more potent. When we utilize force to educate people, it's often rejected or not absorbed properly.

If all you have is a hammer, everything looks like a nail.

—Abraham Maslow, American psychologist

Likewise, people educated to use force when encountering conflict will subconsciously create more conflict. Nelson Mandela said education is the most powerful weapon to change the world.

Every individual has a unique gift and the teacher's path is allowing the student to discover his gift on his own. Dr. Kano was incredibly talented at developing the character of each student into a powerful resource within society. The merging of the Bushido book and the Kodokan dojo led one of the four guardians, Yoshitsugu Yamashita, to become a personal instructor to an American president. Theodore Roosevelt read the Bushido book and was very impressed with both the martial arts aspect and the adjoining philosophy associated with the teachings.

In 1905, Roosevelt offered Yamashita the position of Judo teacher at the U.S. Naval Academy in Annapolis, Maryland, but the academy's instructor, George Grant, resisted the idea. Consequently, a challenge match was scheduled between the two men. Yamashita was over 40 and stood 5' ¼" tall, weighing 149 pounds. Grant was over six feet tall and weighed more than 300 pounds. The match lasted for two minutes of high intensity grappling, as Grant tried to overpower his foe. Yamashita used an arm bar to control Grant and President Roosevelt was so impressed that he appointed Yamashita to the academy as an instructor.

Yamashita was an open-minded martial arts practitioner, always conducting himself with honor and respect. He taught martial arts not just to Roosevelt's wife, but to other upper-class wives associated with the government's administration. One participant was the granddaughter of General Robert E. Lee, leader of the Confederate forces during America's Civil War. Yamashita was a pioneer in offering martial arts instruction to women, utilizing his knowledge that in Judo and Jiu Jitsu size is of less consequence than technique and skill. Yamashita spread Judo to a world-wide audience, his actions a tribute to Dr. Kano's vision of mutual prosperity and the efficient use of energy.

Once a person uncovers his gift, through education and training, the challenge is to utilize it in the most effective way, without getting distracted. A gift can attract attention and popularity and this invites more distraction. With all knowledge comes the responsibility to maximize the sharing of the gift with all who desire it.

Jiu Jitsu may be briefly defined as an application of anatomical knowledge to the purpose of offense or defense. It differs from wrestling, in that it does not depend upon muscular strength. It differs from other forms of attack in that it uses no weapons. Its feat consists in clutching or striking such part of the enemy's body as will make him numb and incapable of resistance. Its object is not to kill, but to incapacitate one for action for the time being.

—Inazo Niobe, from the Bushido book.

A lot of Jiu Jitsu is based around the idea of not hurting people. Jiu Jitsu gives an option to tap or submit. The intention is not to hurt or punish the opponent.

—Demian Maia Jiu Jitsu Black belt, UFC Fighter, ADCC champion.

I see Jiu Jitsu as kinesthetic chess. It requires logical thinking and helps integrate the entire brain. The right side of the brain is for creation and inspiration, while the left is for analyzing and logical thinking. Professor Nitobe and Dr. Kano saw that the cultivation of character from artistic and motor skills activity required a fully-integrated brain. Martial arts can help promote this for the next generation.

At the end of my classes, the kids sit with their knees on the ground, called *Seiza*, and close their eyes for mediation, called *Mokuso*. This is traditional martial arts training to help them calm down from the excitement and adrenalin, and demonstrates how to learn to control your emotions. I teach them that martial arts are only for self-defense purposes outside the academy. One boy's parents told me about how a bully was attacking their child and throwing punches at him, and other bullies were also there, but he managed to defuse the situation without anyone getting hurt. I was very proud of having educated him to have courage and the warrior mindset.

*Gracie family and Machado brothers. Grand Master
(center, seated), Carlos Gracie (left), Helio Gracie (right),
Rigan Machado (6th from right, standing up).*

Chapter 11

The Art of Discipline

Discipline, as a samurai virtue, was traditionally centered in the concept of not allowing one's emotions to show and being in control of your internal reactions regardless of your external reality. If you demonstrated a lack of control, your opponent could take advantage of you. The modern warrior looks at any challenge as an opportunity to grow productively, but it's easy to get trapped by negative emotions. Turning a negative situation into a positive one requires persistence and solid support from like-minded people.

In ancient times, the samurai viewed love as a weaker virtue. From the heart of today's warrior comes a spirit of tenderness and love. Today, we're learning to overcome the fear of expressing gentleness and compassion, and how to view these as strengths. Harnessing this energy and then sharing it with others is a key characteristic of the new era. This requires the mindset of befriending your opponent. A Japanese martial arts expert, Gozo Shioda, described this philosophy as, "…the ultimate martial arts goal is becoming a friend (with the one) who is trying to (beat) you…" When faced with an attack, Shioda's mindset was not disturbed because of his lifelong commitment to training and discipline.

An important part of discipline is the ability to juggle and make priorities. In the act of juggling, some balls are made of glass and some will bounce back like rubber. Total focus and concentration are required to juggle everything. If we become too focused in one area, others are likely to fall and some may break. In my martial arts journey, I was impressed by the mindset of Karate master Joko Ninomiya (founder of Enshin Karate), a living expression of the samurai. His disciplined mindset greatly inspires me when I face a challenging situation.

Master Joko is the father of one of my friends and he is in his sixties, but still trains the same way as when he was young. He believes in consistency—and how dripping water wears away a stone. From him, I've taken my discipline to a different level. Before him, I'd been training every day. But after meeting him, I worked harder to break through own my limitations.

Author with Brazilian Jiu Jitsu Masters.

My Jiu Jitsu mentor, Rigan Machado, also assisted my evolution as a student and then as an instructor. Whenever I lost a match, I felt that I'd dishonored him. He reminded me that winning isn't everything. "If you learned something from this," he said, "it's all good." At the time, I may not have fully appreciated what he meant, but now I understand that competition is a wonderful tool for cultivating the mind and for self-growth.

Musashi Miyamoto, one of Japan's greatest samurai swordsman and the developer of using two swords simultaneously, was also well known for his self-discipline. Musashi mastered the art of painting and calligraphy and was an accomplished writer, publishing the book, *Five Rings (Gorin No Sho)*.

Although he was a great martial artist and a highly-trained artist, writer, and philosopher, his character didn't fit the expectation of the era so the daimyo (feudal lords) found it difficult to hire him as a clan swordsmanship instructor. Instead, he became a legend of discipline by finding his own style and writing a short manual, "Dokkodo (the way of walking alone)." Although he wasn't seen as successful in Japan, Musashi discovered self-realization through the sword and his principles are now timeless.

A Stanford University study in assessing issues of discipline found that children who were able to wait for long-term rewards ended up with more productive life outcomes. The study offered an immediate reward of one treat (a marshmallow, cookie or pretzel) as opposed to two treats fifteen minutes later and discovered that the children able to engage in delayed gratification, when tested later in life, scored better on SAT tests, educational attainment, body mass index, and other measures.

In traditional samurai culture, warriors focused on cultivating their discipline and inner spirit because they were faced with life and death situations. Today, we use these principles to manage ourselves better in every part of our lives.

I've been teaching kids in both Japan and America since 1997. When I started, I followed the Japanese way of discipline, but in the U.S. I realized that some children don't like to be challenged and some parents will let them stay in their comfort zone. The key is finding the right balance. Jiu Jitsu is a long journey and when I see children stay with it and transform themselves through discipline and commitment, I have a lot of respect for them and their parents. The kids show us their true warrior spirits.

Chapter 12

Embracing Life and Death

To understand the certainty that our days are limited—to face this in our lives—is to accept the fragility that is human existence. As a modern warrior, the challenge is to live efficiently and effectively, with the knowledge that our time goes by quickly. Today's warrior discovers that the Bushido code lessons include all the virtues, including living with passion, then recycling our purpose and giving it back to others.

Historically, the practice of *seppuku* (death by the warrior's own hand), was a dramatic example of the acceptance of mortality. Samurai lived out their commitments, cutting open their own stomachs if they failed in their responsibilities or brought shame to their family. This was how to regain honor after what they'd done. They lived inside an extreme regimen, but we've learned from their example and evolved from that. We don't want anyone now thinking that death by his own hands is an inspired act. We still need commitment and to live responsibly, because we'll always have obstacles to break through. But we need to find the right way to use our life force. This mindset encourages us to become more devoted to living with purpose and to spiritual growth.

Because of the ancient warrior's acceptance of the presence of death, the samurai could completely embrace life. For the modern warrior, the challenge is to not waste time or energy unproductively. Dr. Jigoro Kano's phrase *seiryoku zenyo* meant maximum efficiency of energy for potential growth. When we break down the *kanji* (Chinese symbols) of *seiryoku zenyo*, we're looking at transforming potential life force energy into useful expressions of creativity.

The co-founder of Gracie Jiu Jitsu, Helio Gracie, who carried the samurai spirit in Brazil, held strict beliefs regarding sexual energy and optimizing diet and digestion. Ultimately, he was very effective, living and training until 95. When we consider the gift of life, the science and statistics behind conception looks more and more like a miracle.

If we can find a simple appreciation for how we came to be, we're less likely to waste our life energy. Death can become more symbolic than literal, as in the death of a bad habit or a behavior that no longer serves us, by changing our relationship to it. The first law of thermodynamics states that energy can neither be created nor destroyed, but it can be transferred or transformed from one state to another. "Darkness cannot drive out darkness, only light can do that. Hate cannot drive out hate; only love can do that," said Dr. Martin Luther King. If we can let dark habits die, we can make that transformation. Many success stories flow from an individual coming to martial arts and finding a pathway forward and transforming challenging circumstances into a life he or she can be proud of.

Historically, the sword was a reflection of the spirit of the samurai. Today, it stands for a person's regular actions and behaviors. As we polish our character and make good decisions, our sword gets sharpened to cut through any circumstance.

When we look at the meaning of death, we see clearly the bigger picture of life. This gives us a broader perspective versus a single dimensional value.

Life and death are one thread, the same line viewed from different sides.

–Lao Tzu

In combat sports, we usually don't see actual death, but there are still complex issues. One student told me that he still had the fight or flight mindset when he started to train in Jiu Jitsu. He was an Airborne Army survivor from Iraq and many in his troop had died from a bomb explosion. He has PTSD and a psychologist had advised him to do physical activity. He began Jiu Jitsu after coming home from the war because it was very hard for him to adjust to civilian reality. After he trained with me for a while, I saw significant improvement in his mental awareness and connections to his movements. The tension in his body lowered, along with a positive shift in his emotions and thinking patterns. "Jiu Jitsu made me a better human being," he said.

He was raising his four-year-old daughter alone and, with martial arts training, his energy changed. This helped both him and his child. Jiu Jitsu gave him control over his emotions and he became a lovable dad. He brings his daughter to my academy and she'll start Jiu Jitsu soon.

Chapter 13

The Sword: The Soul of the Samurai

The katana sword was born in fire. *Tan ren* means hitting the sword at high heat and creating sparks that reveal that impurities in the metal. The fire drives them out, making the *katana* strong and durable. The forming of a modern warrior is similar; during the heat of struggle, of learning, the impurities of mind are refined. The warrior becomes more precise about how to live in a productive way. Unnecessary behaviors make the sword (and the person) duller. Correct ones help the warrior find peace in any environment.

As a boy learning Kendo, I was trained by a Japanese riot police officer in the art of swordsmanship. The dojo code was, "The samurai sword is your mindset. You must learn the mindset before you learn to use the sword." The sword wasn't just the symbol of the samurai warrior, but displayed his spirit. The highest level of self-control meant not drawing the sword to achieve justice and such actions were a true reflection of the warrior's commitment to self and others.

Katsu Kaishu, a great hero of Japanese samurai during the Edo period, possessed a deep reverence for life. "I despise killing and have never killed a man," he said. "I used to keep [my sword] tied so tightly to my scabbard that I couldn't draw the blade even if I had wanted to." Kaishu was well known for finding practical methods to resolve conflict and was a mentor to Dr. Kano and influenced Professor Nitobe, who revolutionized what it meant to be a samurai in changing times.

Known as Count Katsu, he also said, "The best won victory is that obtained without shedding of blood…the ultimate ideal of knighthood is peace." Although he was the object of repeated assassination attempts, he never tarnished his sword with blood. During the Meiji restoration, Katsu helped give Japan a more productive future and advised Dr. Kano on how to invest in the Kodokan and Japanese education system. "A diploma from your school may make you secure for a time," Dr. Kano said, "but cannot make you secure forever. The only thing that can truly make you secure forever is your actual ability."

Kodokan. Birth place of Judo. Tokyo, Japan.

In the past, there was a concept known as a life-giving sword, which means cutting through ideas that only serve ourselves. We can be on the correct side of a conflict, but if we're stubborn or complain about the other side, we're not using our energy productively. That energy should be focused not on the opponent, but on how to resolve the issue. As Dr. Kano said, "What is the point of complaining? It is certainly no fun for those who have to listen to the complaints. The energy used to make unpleasant complaints can certainly not be considered *seiryoku zenyo* (maximum efficiency of productive energy)." As we cut ineffective ties, we connect to a way of life that brings us closer to our goals.

In martial arts, we're learning techniques that can hurt people. We must, therefore, be aware of and have a deep respect for the art and the honor that accompanies our skills. When we impart the correct knowledge, it's a transaction of spirit that doesn't die with us, but flourishes in the future. What we accomplish as individuals affects the larger community and while our own existence is limited, the sharing of this spirit becomes unlimited in potential. The samurai sword can be used for good or bad, the same as a gun or knife. If a chef has the knife, it's a productive tool that will lead to one enjoying a meal. If utilized by a negative mindset, the result can be fatal. Used properly, it can lead to self-realization. As Musashi said, "There is nothing outside of yourself that can enable you to get better, richer, stronger or smarter. Everything is within…Seek nothing outside of yourself."

Today, the warrior spirit can be embodied by any race, gender or age—not the case in the past, inside a feudal system with a caste you were either born or married into. Back then, one mistake could cost you your life.

On my martial arts path, I've made mistakes, but I've learned as much from losing as from winning. In the end, these mistakes gave me more understanding of who I am and more inner strength. A famous quote in Japan is, "Fall down seven times, get up eight. Always rising after a fall."

Every time you get up you uncover more of your own strength and your own long journey. In Karate training, I discovered the words of Musashi Minamoto, a well-known samurai who was never defeated: "The way of martial arts begins with one thousand days. And the true martial arts training starts after ten thousand days."

When I first came to America, I wanted to be strong like a samurai sword, but I faced great challenges and made missteps. I didn't yet understand the making of these swords, which is similar to how martial arts training can shape our warrior spirit. To become stronger, the sword must be heated and banged to reach a purified state. Without this process, it's fragile and breakable and we can't use it when we need to. Being forged in fire is how we gain the inner strength to find a new version of ourselves.

Author teaching a kids' class.

Chapter 14

The Female Warrior

Tsuyoku, Yasashiku, Utsukushiku
Be strong, be gentle, be beautiful, in mind, body and spirit.

—Keiko Fukuda, *Kodokan* Judo, 9th degree Black belt,
granddaughter of Dr. Kano's Jiu Jitsu teacher

Female samurai warriors often fought on the battlefield as fiercely as their male counterparts. They were trained to defend themselves and their families at home, while the male was away at war, and they too possessed the mindset of Bushido code. The evolution of female potential and inner power has often been depicted in the popular culture role of the princess. Modern princesses in movies by Disney and Hayao Miyazaki embody the independence and strength needed to overcome whatever obstacles are in her way, while being kind to people, animals, and the environment.

Kime-No-Kata (Martial Arts Form training) by female Kodokan practitioners Ayako Akutagawa (left) and Masako Noritomi (right).

© Kodokan Judo Institute.

After the publication of the Bushido book, President Theodore Roosevelt decided to receive personal martial arts training from Yoshitsugu Yamashita, one of the four Guardians of the Kodokan. He's considered to be the pioneering forerunner of teaching women martial arts in the U.S. Dr. Kano also understood women's potential and privately practiced with his wife to refine how the art could flourish publicly for females. In modern times, *Sensei* Keiko Fukuda's quote at the start of this chapter can be seen as an ideal template for anyone, regardless of gender.

Be Strong in mind, body, and spirit. The power of the female warrior is like that of bamboo, strong yet supple. At first sight, the bamboo's strength is not obvious. Once you touch it, its strength becomes more apparent, but if you touch too hard, its flexibility redirects the force. Many highly-skilled martial artists focus on developing this kind of strength.

Be gentle in mind, body and spirit. The emotional sensitivity developed by the female warrior is precise and intuitive, yet regulated. The Japanese phrase, *mei kyo shi sui,* means a bright mirror that reflects the world, but is not affected by it. Through training, the natural emotions and intuition become razor sharp and polished, ready to be applied in everyday life.

Be beautiful in mind, body, and spirit: Real beauty is timeless and comes from within. Through training and self-realization, we find the beauty of who we are for as long as we're alive.

In the early 20th century, a group of British women known as suffragettes fought for the right to vote. They faced great opposition, often in the form of violence, and the group learned Jiu Jitsu/Judo as a means of self-defense. Their motto was, "Deeds, not words," which is in alignment with martial arts. In 1928, because of their efforts, all women in England earned the right to vote. Recent times have shown a dramatic shift in human understanding of what a female warrior is. While physical strength is important, the female warrior is equipped (mentally and emotionally) to face and overcome challenging circumstances and stigmas, which have prevented empowerment.

When you admire something about another woman, tell her.
Get into the habit of lifting each other up.

—Unknown.

In my martial arts journey, I've met so many different types of female warriors: world-level athletes, female martial artists, etc. One of my friends, a former Judo Olympian, always displays her fortitude and inner strength when we train. She reminds me of the word *Ossu.* In the martial arts community, we use this as a greeting. It means even if your obstacles are bigger and stronger than you, you'll find a way forward.

Sometimes, parents bring their girls to me to give them the strength to deal with bullies. They have to confront their challenges emotionally and physically to break through their comfort zones and get a stronger version of themselves. I see their small steps forward, but really they are huge steps in their lives. Little by little, they gain confidence and inner strength, and it is greatly rewarding for me to see them change and grow.

Every person, male or female, faces his or her own level of stress, and I have to respect that as a teacher. We all grow in different ways, using our culture, gender, beliefs, and circumstances. For this reason, I rely on Dr. Kano's quote, "If there is effort, there is always accomplishment."

I see differences between the male and female warrior mindset, but they are good differences. Generally, women are sensitive to emotions, but have strong minds. Some men are also sensitive, but the traditional samurai culture didn't talk about feelings because it came from a history of war. Jiu Jitsu now opens the door to everyone to find his or her own way to express the warrior spirit.

Two girls sparing at kids' class.

Chapter 15

The Future of Bushido

The samurai code was born from the chaos of ancient Japan to become what we know today. The key to the code is for each individual to know the correct self and mindset as they strive to master the nuances of life. As Conde Koma/Mitsuyo Maeda said during his years of competition, "Find yourself." A well-known quote from *kyudo*, the art of archery, says, "When shooting, sometimes we will hit the target but miss the self. At other times, we will miss the target, but hit the self. Our purpose, though, is to hit the target as the self and hope that the sharp sound of arrow penetrating paper will awaken us from the so-called 'dream of life' and give us real insight into the ultimate state of being."

We cannot forget the lessons of the past and how they merge into the present. Bushido is grounded in ancient samurai wisdom and while it may seem old-fashioned the code today is for a journey into a higher purpose and to shape our responses when we face conflict. We now have access to so much wisdom from our predecessors all over the world, but the challenge is how to best use it. The goal is to utilize the Bushido code and remain unaffected when we encounter conflict. Dr. Kano wrote about this quality as being the way of education: *tenku kai katsu* means to be like the sky/universe/ocean—formless, limitless, and unaffected.

Dr. Kano is teaching a future generation.
© Kodokan Judo Institute

From birth we face conflict and today we live in a world where all cultures and all peoples coexist. In the 1964 Olympics in Tokyo, the Dutch *judoka* Antonius Geesink won gold against his Japanese opponent. Geesink's coaches wanted to come on the mat to celebrate his victory, but he humbly told them to be reserved. His calm behavior was a tribute to Dr. Kano's lifelong mission of sharing Bushido culture to the world through Olympic sports.

"Sport has the power to change the world," said Nelson Mandela. "It has the power to inspire. It has the power to unite people in a way that little else does. It speaks to youth in a language they understand. Sport can create hope where once there was only despair. It is more powerful than government in breaking down racial barriers."

Conflict inevitably is a consequence of miscalculation and mistakes. Dr. Kano understood that education was a potent tool to work through our differences. For this reason, Katsu Kaishu saw Dr. Kano as a samurai in a time when they no longer carried the sword. Professor Nitobe respected what Kaishu Katsu did in negotiating the bloodless surrender of Edo Castle (July, 1868) as indicative of the productive ways of peace. With our global culture and mass weapons of destruction, this goal is more important now than in ancient times. The world is consistently moving, evolving, and changing so we always need to adjust to it.

Technology advances every day and while it can be used productively to help people, we must also understand its dark side. Blindly relying on technology and artificial intelligence or being engulfed by virtual reality is known in Japan as *ukiyo-e* (floating world), a genre of artwork that depicted the hedonistic tendencies of living a dream within a dream. We must see the value of technology, but use it wisely, as every previous generation has had to use the tools available to it.

In their time, Dr. Kano and Professor Nitobe worked hard to share Bushido to create peace and prosperity, just as *Sensei* Maeda lived his unique way to build for the greater good. Nitobe believed that the power of the code "will not perish"—if we train ourselves to find more choices in conflict, beyond fight or flight.

In 1900, he did not envision that in 1964 Judo would become an Olympic event, creating an international interest in martial arts. This helped people embrace warrior training and the idea of maximum efficiency for the mutual benefit of all, on and off the mat. I believe that the Bushido code will continue to evolve, despite the vastly different cultures of our world. This evolutionary process incorporates all of our modern and ever-increasing technology. The Internet and what it is yet to become will further enhance the search for knowledge and understanding. The need for regulating oneself and maintaining respectful connections to others becomes more and more vital. As humans, we have the tendency to use technology in destructive ways, so we need to awaken to a different state of mind.

The way of the warrior is the discipline to choose light over dark.

Professor Nitobe would be greatly encouraged at how the code has influenced other cultures beyond Japan's. I'm grateful to be able to share Professor Nitobe's vision in this book and to thank Master Rigan Machado for inspiring me in the direction of self-discovery.

I'm also grateful to Master Jean Jacques Machado, (Master Rigan's younger brother) for giving me additional insight into how Bushido evolved with the Gracie family in Brazil. That family allowed me to appreciate Jiu Jitsu as a way of life, which inspired me to trace it back to Kodokan Judo. I came to greatly appreciate my own journey out of Japan and immersing myself in foreign cultures. The conclusion of my journey with this book brought me back to the origins of Jiu Jitsu: the Kodokan Judo institute. I want to thank *Sensei* Naoki Murata (8th dan Judo and author) and *Sensei* Motonari Sameshima (8th dan former Olympic Judo coach). During my visit there, they helped me understand how Judo offers great tools to benefit the self and the world.

My commitment is to support the evolutionary process wherein all who become students will also become teachers and participants in a future filled with both challenges and the power and potential for global change. We cannot imagine what the future holds, but our goal is to polish our character through physical activity, with a correct template for behavior. As technology and biotechnology continue to advance, our responsibility is to oversee its development within our own development. Our core challenge is to remain centered no matter what the future may hold.

I always enjoy talking with the younger generation or with those who live or work in a different culture. From meeting people everywhere, I see the "warrior in the garden" concept as useful for everyone. I've had the opportunity to share the art in Israel, a country surrounded by conflict. One day I rode with my Israeli friends from Tel Aviv to the Dead Sea and was around many people on active duty in military and a combat training instructor. We all got along very well and I saw how martial arts bring people together with no boundaries created by religion, politics or background. Near the Israeli border was a bomb shelter for people to escape an attack. The Jiu Jitsu academy I visited in Eliat was also inside a bomb shelter. It made me think about how there's more to martial arts than earning points or winning matches. Sometimes, we put too much focus on just winning. Martial arts can teach us how to redirect our energy to avoid conflict and steer us in the direction of peace.

I took some courses in Military Krav Maga, the martial arts of the Israeli Defense Forces (IDF), and the Israeli security forces martial arts. Krav Maga is an eclectic combination of techniques adopted from boxing, wrestling, Aikido, Judo, Jiu Jitsu, and Karate. It combines sports and self-defense. Because of Israel's real-world situation in the Middle East, an immediate urgency is present, even during training, making everything more realistic.

If we can use martial arts to teach the younger generation peace, it will make the training more meaningful for everyone. We do this by teaching self-control and not allowing certain dangerous movements, groin or eye attacks, small joint manipulations, etc. A well-known samurai swords-manship master Musashi Minamoto said, "There is more than one path to the top of the mountain."

Being flexible in all things goes beyond winning and losing. Stay open-minded to meeting all kinds of warriors in any community: artists, writers, musicians, sports figures, and anyone involved in facing challenging, creative work. All are warriors in the garden. Life is short, so take the action to be better than yesterday and do so in a humble way. The garden will continue to grow and flourish.

Bushido held that interest of the family and
of the members thereof is intact, one and inseparable.

—Inazo Nitobe, from Bushido chapter on Loyalty

Afterword

First, I want to thank you the reader for supporting this book. Ten per cent of its profits will go to Doctors without Borders. Partial profits will go to Awaken (a 501c3 non-profit) to support the next generation that utilizes modern Bushido.

Special thanks to Master Rigan who helped me to understand Jiu Jitsu is more than just a combat system. It was interesting to see samurai culture travel the world and to learn to appreciate the variations of modern warriors. Master Rigan advised me to write this book and while it seemed far-fetched, I'm grateful for my journey as an author, which brought me many realizations about my own development. Thanks to Master Crolin Gracie for sharing the story how Conde Koma from Kodokan, Japan influenced his dad Grand Master Carlos Gracie with his Bushido in Brazil.

Thanks to Master Jean Jacques Machado who gave me advice about the way of Jiu Jitsu. This took me to Kodokan Institute, where I was exposed to physical education for Bushido, Thanks to Sensei Murata and Sensei Sameshima from Kodokan. There are so many teachers, including predecessors, I want to thank for being part of this work. Thanks to all my training partners and opponents who presented me the opportunity for challenges and growth. Thanks to all my students and friends.

In samurai culture, they don't usually talk about family in public, but I want to thank my parents who allowed me to pursue my passion in a different country. Thanks to my siblings who've always supported me. And thanks to my daughter who every day made me a better (dad) human instead of a wild samurai.

A special thanks to Mike Ninomiya. I couldn't have finished this book without him. We spent many hours together during the nearly three years it took to complete.

Thank you.

Cover photography: Minh Bui

Book Cover design: Tracy Van Dolder, Virtually Possible Designs

Editorial Director: Stephen Singular

Editor: Val Anisimow

Copy Editors: Adam Clark and Robert Lee Shaw

Consultant: Mike Ninomiya

Book Layout: Gail Nelson

Photo credit: Kodokan Judo Institute, Nitobe Memorial Museum, Bui Pix

Made in the
USA
Columbia, SC